PAULINE TAI

Editor
Investor's Scorecard
Money Magazine

Mastering Money Matters

PRENTICE HALL, ENGLEWOOD CLIFFS, NEW JERSEY 07632

Library of Congress Cataloging-in-Publication Data

Tai, Pauline.   (Date)
    Mastering money matters.
    Includes index.
    1. Finance, Personal. I. Title.
HG179.T33 1988   332.024   87-30035
ISBN   0-13-560062-6

Editorial/production supervision: Gretchen K. Chenenko
Cover design: Lundgren Graphics, Ltd.
Manufacturing buyer: Rick Washburn

The publisher offers discounts on this book when ordered in
bulk quantities. For more information, write:

  Special Sales/College Marketing
  Prentice Hall
  College Technical and Reference Division
  Englewood Cliffs, New Jersey 07632

© 1988 by Pauline Tai
Published by Prentice-Hall, Inc.
A Division of Simon & Schuster
Englewood Cliffs, New Jersey 07632

Printed in the United States of America

10 9 8 7 6 5 4 3 2 1

ISBN   0-13-560062-6

Prentice-Hall International (UK) Limited, *London*
Prentice-Hall of Australia Pty. Limited, *Sydney*
Prentice-Hall Canada Inc., *Toronto*
Prentice-Hall Hispanoamericana, S.A., *Mexico*
Prentice-Hall of India Private Limited, *New Delhi*
Prentice-Hall of Japan, Inc., *Tokyo*
Simon & Schuster Asia Pte. Ltd., *Singapore*
Editora Prentice-Hall do Brasil, Ltda., *Rio de Janeiro*

For
Aunt Margaret

Contents

Preface

One of the greatest pleasures I get out of my work as a reporter is the opportunities it gives me to chat with people from all walks of life about what concerns and bothers them. Being a generalist at heart, it was natural that when I used to work at the *Wall Street Journal* and now at *Money,* I'm the person who gets many of the more unusual calls and letters that come in from our readers. As a result, I've had lots of opportunities to find out what's on their mind. What's amazing is it's not only the individual investors who need help but also the experts. Often all they need is a source to contact so they can get all the facts, or more common still, to have someone knowledgeable to talk to and to ask questions about what is confusing or bothering them.

At the rate new investment vehicles have been increasing in recent years, it's getting harder and harder to keep up to date with what's going on out there. At the same time, as the electronic media comes of age, everything seems to be changing faster than ever before. Instead of just being concerned with ourselves, American investors must now learn to look outward. As recent events have shown, what happens in Tokyo or Teheran also affects New York and Kansas City. In a shrinking world, we grow ever more interdependent. The international financial markets are irrevocably interrelated. So yesterday's investing strategies just won't work in today's climate.

For example, not very long ago—possibly in our grandparents' days—it was often the practice to invest for the really long term. It was not unusual to have shares such as AT&T or Exxon being owned by a family for generations.

Today, it'd be quite unwise to simply just put away some shares and forget them. To make the most of what you have requires some monitoring—some managing—at least periodically in order to adjust your strategies to deal with the changing circumstances.

Even people who can afford professional help are beginning to realize that it's to their advantage to know the basics for, in the end, they still must make the final decision. The more I chatted with these people, the more I realized there must be something I could do to help them.

The result is this personal financial planning primer, a how-to guide that informs and imparts the pertinent facts, including, where appropriate, the pros and cons. But most important of all, it will ask lots of questions to make you think and, hopefully, understand how things apply to you personally, what to expect, and if all that will fit in with your own temperament and lifestyle. In short, it will be a step-by-step guide to knowing thyself. But instead of simply telling you what to do, it's my hope that the book is done in such a way that it is more like having a friend to talk to so you can decide for yourself what makes most sense.

Along the way, you'll develop a special knack of looking at your own financial situation, not as isolated transactions, but as a whole, much like a jigsaw puzzle where all the pieces fit perfectly. Any individual transaction, you'll soon discover, tends to have some effect on your whole financial well-being, some good and some bad, and often a little of both. The trick is to know how much of each so you can decide which will work best for you.

For example, if you buy a house, you'll soon discover it will put a big crimp in your cash flow, but on the other hand, there'll be some tax advantages. You can deduct the mortgage interest, for one, from your federal income taxes, and hopefully you'll be building up some equity so when it's time to sell, you'll realize sizeable gains.

HOW TO USE THIS BOOK

Most chapters in this book contain three parts. The primer, a quick introduction to the concepts of personal financial planning, gives you information about what's out there and how to apply it to your own situation. The source list covers all the places where you can go for help, as well as how you can learn more about what takes your fancy. The aim here is not to inundate you with tons of data but simply to whet your appetite so you'll want to proceed to the next course with relish— and, maybe even decide to take the first step by getting organized.

To help you towards that goal, interspersed in the appropriate chapters will be tables with sample forms for you to complete. When these are completed, you'll have at your finger tips most of the important facts you'll need to make the appropriate decision.

I hope you will have as much fun reading and using this book as I had in writing it for you.

Acknowledgments

Through the years, I have interviewed numerous money managers and other financial experts. I have learned much from them. Many of these same people contributed most generously in time and patience to make this book a reality. A good number of them also read the manuscript for accuracy. For all their help, I thank them from the bottom of my heart.

I'd like to mention, in particular, James B. Cloonan, American Association of Individual Investors; David Dreman, Dreman Embry Inc.; Loren Dunton, National Center for Financial Education; Paul Havemann, HSH Associates; Robert Heady, Bank Rate Monitor; Thomas J. Herzfeld, Thomas J. Herzfeld Advisors; Yale Hirsch, The Hirsch Organization; Richard Johannesen, Salomon Brothers; Bob Levy and Spero Kripotos, CDA Investment Technologies.

Also, Jean Barkhorn, *Town & Country;* Joe Guilfoyle, *Wall Street Journal;* Ed Henry, *Changing Times;* Stanley Cohen, Moseley Securities; Edward Muhlenfeld, Rauscher Pierce Refsnes; Ben Zacks, Zacks Investment Research; Monte Helme, Century 21 Real Estate Corporation; National Association of Realtors; Investment Company Institute; Laura Berger, No-Load Fund Association; Hedda Nadler, Mount & Nadler; H. Spencer Nilson and David Robertson, *The Nilson Report;* Sylvester J. Schieber, The Wyatt Company; Joe Schlussel, The

Diamond Registry; Bill Brennan, The Brennan Report; Bill Wilson and Marion Marshall, Tax Foundation; and Joyce Orsini, New York State Savings & Loan Association.

In addition, a special thank you to Bernard Barnett, Seidman & Seidman; Stephen B. Rodner, Pryor Cashman Sherman Flynn; and to *Money* Magazine's managing editor, Landon Y. Jones, and executive editor Frank Lalli for their interest and generous support.

To William Clabby of the *Wall Street Journal*, who gave me my first chance in financial journalism, I owe my deepest appreciation. Without his guidance and encouragement, none of this would have been possible.

Last but certainly not least, I'd like to thank those friends and family members who took the time from their very hectic schedules to read the manuscript and made many useful suggestions. I thank, in particular, Pat, who spent precious weekends proofreading this book; and Rosemarie and Tom, without whose technical assistance, I probably never would have gone this far with my IBM system.

P. T.

Foreword

Money magazine, where I work, has assembled over the years the finest collection of personal finance and investing journalists in the world. Most of them tend to have specialties—insurance, estate planning, Wall Street, and so on. Whenever I have a question I know who to turn to for an informed answer.

And now you have an authority to turn to with your personal finance questions—this excellent primer by Pauline Tai, who not coincidentally is the Investor's Scorecard editor of *Money* magazine.

Ms. Tai is an extraordinary talent. Born in China, raised in Hong Kong, educated there and the United States, she is multilingual and multifaceted, with a special affinity for classical music and financial statistics. Just as aspiring novelists fall in love with words, she is a financial journalist who fell for numbers. She says, "Numbers are my friends." That grounding in facts gives her reporting a special accuracy. Beyond that, she has an uncanny ability to put herself in the average reader's place and gather the information needed to help the reader reach reasonable conclusions.

Ms. Tai has produced a simple-to-follow map to financial security, beginning with the questions you should ask yourself to clarify your personal goals and followed by chapters that will help you figure out what your true financial standing is and how you actually spend your money. There is also a separate section on credit that has clear and timely tips on how to avoid borrowing any more than you really must, which is a timely strategy in this tax-reform era.

For many, much of the most valuable information will be found in the section on investing. She calls it the smorgasbord of investments, and it is a first-rate, fact-filled primer loaded with the proper fundamentals that even sophisticated investors will find useful to review: What is the best place to put your savings now? What strategies should you adopt if interest rates decline? Are tax-exempt bonds a good idea for you? (One of the many tables in this book spells out exactly what you would get after taxes).

The same thoughtful approach is used in reviewing stock investments, complete with a table of the estimated future earnings of all 30 stocks that make up the Dow Jones Industrial Average. She hasn't forgotten gems or coins, either. You'll see, for example, why rubies rather than diamonds should be a girl's best friend. And you'll learn that when it comes to gold coins, Pandas may outfly Eagles.

Mutual funds are becoming increasingly popular. Here you will find a concise introduction on how to evaluate the many available fund choices. Besides a complete table of the current top-performing international funds, there is a rundown of eight large funds that have performed admirably in advancing markets as well as declining ones.

The book concludes with sample portfolios for persons with various objectives. No one can foretell the future. But these tables, based on historic performance, are the next best thing. Not only do you see what your annual rate of return will be over the next five years, but also the amount of deviation from that rate you are likely to experience, depending on the type of portfolio you choose. For example, a 100% stock portfolio may return up to 24% a year, give or take 10%, while a corporate bond portfolio will throw off 11%, give or take 5%. Using these statistical projections, even beginning investors can easily assemble a model investment portfolio tailored to their desired return and the amount of risk they are willing to accept. And as if that wasn't enough, Ms. Tai goes beyond it by including quick checklists and suitable model portfolios for individuals in each stage of their life.

If you are now ready to get organized, there is also a comprehensive workbook for personal information—available by mail—that will save you hours of time when you have to fill out all those inevitable financial forms bankers, insurers, and government bureaucrats keep sticking under your nose. Every date and statistic can be at your finger tips. What a joy!

When it comes to individual financial planning, what more could you ask?

Frank Lalli
Executive Editor
Money Magazine

Know Thyself

DIFFERENT SEASONS, DIFFERENT NEEDS

In life's changing seasons, you'll be faced with innumerable challenges as well as different needs to fulfill and new goals to meet. We may all be individuals with our own free will. But as human beings sharing the same world, we all go through the same life cycle. At different seasons, we're called upon to play different roles. Sometimes we even get to repeat the same roles but at another season. Let's start with the master script from the beginning.

Spring

This is the season when all things in nature burst forth with new life. First, the leaves, and with the proper care, then buds will appear, which eventually will turn into lovely blooms. So it is with our own life. An infant with loving nurturing will grow into a healthy child and later on into a young adult. In an ideal world, childhood should be a carefree happy period. Unfortunately, in our industrialized world, we're increasingly forcing our children to be grownups before their time.

Summer

Summer is when life is in full bloom and young adults graduate and enter the real world of work. For many, it's a time to start building on their profession, earn some money, fall in love, get married and have kids. It's also a time to start accumulating assets and set some aside for a rainy day.

Autumn

When leaves turn to red and gold before falling off completely, it is autumn. For matured adults, this is a time for winding down—the kids should now be primarily on their own—so it's a time to think and do more for yourself again. But this is getting to be easier said than done, since in this modern society, we're discovering that just when our children are leaving, our aging parents may need our help—either financially, physically, or both. In addition, it's also a time to start preparing the practical aspects of our own retirement.

Winter

Ideally, this is a time to hibernate, to rejuvenate, to do what you've always wanted to, but never had the time or the resources to do it. It's a time to enjoy and to share the good things in life with family and friends. With some thoughtful consideration and planning, it's possible to make this a reality.

The in-between seasons

Real life, however, is usually not as straight forward as nature's script. In postindustrialized America, the family is going through some drastic changes. Along with more options, both men and women are also called upon to play more roles—roles that are often no longer very well defined. For example, as an increasing number of women join the work force, there will be many more two-income families. Women are already having children later—if they have any at all. With one in four marriages ending in divorce, there will be many more second families. The advancement in medical technology and care means better health and longer life expectancy for most people. With the greying of America, there are fewer young workers to provide sufficient funding for social security. For many, the only solution is to work longer or to start a second career. All this adds up to a muddying of the seasons, and the in-between seasons will play an increasingly larger role in our lives.

Some of us may take longer to get from one stage to the next, or we may even have the seasons reversed. Some may repeat seasons, or skip one altogether. Most of us go through life without giving the seasons much thought. We expect things to simply happen at the appropriate time. As more choices become available, it may be necessary to give the seasons some thought, especially if you want to make the most of them. Otherwise, there's always the possibility that if we're not careful, we may end up being in between seasons all our life.

Most major decisions we have to face in this adventure through the circle of life demand that we must first truly get to know ourselves—what it is that we really want. So it is with investment decisions. Before you can decide whether to put your money in stocks or bonds or mutual funds, you must first find out who you are, how comfortable you are with risk, and what you want to accomplish.

EIGHT QUESTIONS TO HELP YOU GET IN TOUCH
WITH YOURSELF

Here are eight questions to ask yourself that will help you sort out your ideas and feelings.

1. What temperament are you? Are you adventurous and like to take chances? Or are you the exact opposite and tend to dislike uncertainties? If you have a taste for gambling, then a stock market in great flux will give you great pleasure. But on the other hand, if you dislike such ups-and-downs, it's a sure way to become a nervous wreck.

2. What lifestyle suits you? Are you a city person? Or do you prefer the suburbs or the countryside? How you live will depend, to a large extent, on your temperament and will definitely have a big effect on how you'll spend or save your money.

3. How much risk do you like to take? Some of us thrive on risks, while others abhor the slightest bit. The idea here then is to get to know your own threshhold so you can search for investments to suit your own risk levels.

4. What job situation do you prefer—being your own boss or working for someone else? Being self-employed requires taking a certain amount of risk and being involved in all facets of a business. You need to be a leader rather than a follower. On the other hand, being employed means security to a certain degree—you're paid a certain amount to do a certain job. You don't have to worry about the bottom line or how you're going to pay your employees.

5. What are your objectives? Nothing gets done unless you have a plan. So it is with investing. Generally, it's good to have some objectives that are short term so you can see some results relatively soon; and then some long-term ones as a means of planning for the future. For example, if you're just starting out, your first goal is to save for an emergency fund. After that, it's time to accumulate assets so one day you can begin investing seriously.

6. How much work do you want to do yourself? Some of us find the details of managing our own money fascinating, while

others find it a boring and tedious task and would prefer never to have to face it.

7. Should you manage your own money or let someone else do it for you? If your answer to question 6 is none, then chances are you should get someone else to manage your money for you. But whether you'll be able to find such a person to do it for you depends mainly on how much money you have. If it's too small an amount, chances are you'll have to cope with it yourself anyway.

8. Who can you go to for help? Who you'll turn to depends on what you need done. For example, if you need a financial checkup, you'll probably go to a financial planner and get a proper plan. On the other hand, if you just want to sell or buy some stocks, you can go to a broker—even a discount one—if you don't need research assistance. If you have substantial assets, you may want to hire an investment advisor to manage your portfolio. For tax queries or planning, you'll go to an accountant, and for legal matters you'll go to a lawyer.

Table 1.1 shows at a quick glance what these five professionals can do for you and at what price.

TABLE 1.1 What professional help may cost you

Profession	What They Can Do For You	At What Price
Accountant	Tax planning Filing Tax returns	$40–150/hour
Broker	Buying/selling, advice	Varies greatly; for example, for 100 shares at $50 each, commission might range from a low of $35 (discount) to a high of $99.50 (full fee).
Full fee/ discount	Buying and selling only	
Financial planner Fee basis/ commission	A generalist who knows the overall picture and can do two things for you: draw up a financial plan and implement it for you. However, you may opt to	Varying ways; $40–150 an hour; more likely, a flat fee (from a few hundred to thousands of dollars) for the plan; some will combine the fee with

TABLE 1.1 *(Cont.)*

Profession	What They Can Do For You	At What Price
	separate the two steps by having one person to do the plan, who will get a flat fee; and others, who are on commission to do the trading. The argument for this strategy is that those on a fee basis may have less chance of conflicts of interest.	commissions for implementing the plan; some will also charge an annual maintenance fee.
Lawyer Generalist/ specialist	The family lawyer covers all legal matters, while the specialists are consulted for specific issues, such as divorce, or estate planning.	$50–500/hour

TAKING THE NEXT STEP: WHERE TO GET HELP

Tables 1.2 lists resources that can provide you with further information or assistance.

TABLE 1.2

Source	What's Available
FINANCIAL PLANNING	
Institute of Certified Financial Planners 2 Denver Highlands 10065 East Harvard Ave. Denver, CO 80231 (303) 751-7600	Members who successfully complete the course given by the College of Financial Planning, a part of the institute, are entitled to the initials, C.F.P. after their names. You may request a list of members nearest you.
International Association for Financial Planning 2 Concourse Parkway Atlanta, GA 30328 (404) 395-1605	Request the Registry of Financial Planning Practitioners, which lists only those IAFP members with planning experience and specialized training.

TABLE 1.2 *(Cont.)*

Source	What's Available
National Center for Financial Education 50 Fremont San Francisco, CA 94105 (415) 777-0460	The chief goal of this nonprofit membership outfit is to educate and motivate people to save, invest, and plan for their financial future. For a $50 yearly fee, you get a monthly newsletter, a quarterly magazine, and a variety of services to help you get started.

GENERAL FINANCIAL
PUBLICATIONS

Source	What's Available
Barron's Dow Jones & Co. 200 Liberty St. New York, NY 10281 (212) 416-2000	A national business and financial weekly available at newsstands on Saturdays at $1.50 an issue.
Business Week McGraw Hill Inc. 1221 Avenue of the Americas New York, NY 10020 (800) 257-5112	A weekly covering the nation's business; available by subscription or at newsstands.
Changing Times The Kiplinger Washington Editors Inc. 1729 H St. NW Washington, D.C. 20006 (202) 887-6400	A monthly covering topics of interest to the consumer—from cars and computers to stocks, bonds and taxes. A year's subscription is $15 ($2.25/copy at newsstands).
The Economist Subscription Department P. O. Box 904 Farmingdale, NY 11737 (800) 227-5782	A business and financial weekly published in London. The coverage of both *The Economist* and *The Financial Times* (listed next) tends to be more international in scope than American publications. 30 issues for $45 ($2.50/copy at newsstands).
The Financial Times of London 14 East 60th St. New York, NY 10021 (212) 752-4500	A daily now also available in the U.S. the same day at newsstands, $.50 a copy.
Forbes Forbes Inc. 60 Fifth Ave. New York, NY 10011 (212) 620-2200	A business and financial biweekly, except for two weeks in April and in October when it is weekly. $39 a year ($3/copy).

TABLE 1.2 *(Cont.)*

Source	What's Available
Investor Daily P.O. Box 25970 Los Angeles, CA 90025 (213) 477-1453	A new entry in daily financial newspapers aimed specifically at technical investors who use charts extensively in their research.
Money Time, Inc. 1271 Avenue of the Americas New York, NY 10020 (212) 586-1212	A monthly how-to personal finance magazine available at newsstands or by subscription, $31.95 for 13 issues a year ($2.95/copy).
The Wall Street Journal Dow Jones & Co. 200 Liberty St. New York, NY 10281 (212) 416-2000	Increasingly this national financial daily is covering news from around the world, which makes it all the more interesting and useful. Available Monday through Friday. $.50/copy at newsstands.
INVESTMENT ADVISERS	
Investment Counsel Association of America 50 Broad St. New York, NY 10004 (212) 344-0999	Substantial investors in search of an adviser may want to get a list of investment managers who are members of this association. To be cost effective, most managers today set rather high minimums—often $1 million and up.
Hutton Select Managers E.F. Hutton & Co. 824 Market Street Wilmington, DE 19801 (302) 573-5800	Lesser investors ($100,000 or more) may turn to this consulting service to find a money manager. Fees start at 3% of assets and decrease to 1.7% for accounts in excess of $2 million.
INVESTMENT CLUBS	
American Association of Individual Investors 612 N. Michigan Ave. Chicago, IL 60611 (312) 280-0170	Started in 1979, this nonprofit educational group currently has 108,000 members. An annual membership fee of $48 will entitle you to various publications, plus seminars and study groups at reduced costs. Also available is a six-hour video course on investing fundamentals ($95 for members, $129 for others).

TABLE 1.2 *(Cont.)*

Source	What's Available
National Association of Investors P.O. Box 220 Royal Oak, MI 48068 (313) 543-0612	Originally called the National Association of Investment Clubs, this is a nonprofit, largely volunteer organization of investors, where you can get tips on how to invest or help to start your own club.

LEGAL SERVICES

Source	What's Available
American Bar Association American Bar Center 1155 East 60th St. Chicago, IL 60637 (312) 947-4000	Consumer information on such topics as how to choose a lawyer, and the legal aspects of consumer credit, bankruptcy, or marriage. To complain or to get a list of lawyers from the lawyer referral service, you'll have to go through your nearest city, county, or state bar association.
Legal Aid and Legal Services Corp.	Legal Aid and Legal Services offices, numbering more than 1,000, around the country, offer free legal services to those who meet financial eligibility requirements. Some common problems handled by these offices include landlord–tenant, credit, and family issues such as divorce, adoption, social security, and welfare. For an office nearest you check your telephone directory.

TAXES
See Table 4.18 for sources.

What
Are You Worth?

To answer this question properly requires doing two things: taking an inventory of your income and expenses and then comparing what you own with what you owe. This is not really as complicated a task as it has been made out to be. The first time you do it will take some thinking, a little time, and information about what to include in the various components. After that, you need to update it only periodically. That way, you'll always be au courant with your own finances.

INCOME VERSUS OUTGO

Knowing exactly how much you earn and how much you spend each year is the first step to financial planning.

Income includes salaries, dividends on investments, interest on savings account, as well as tips, rents, royalties, pension, or annuity payments.

Outgo includes all expenses such as those for taxes (for example, federal, state, and social security), housing (mortgage, real-estate taxes, utilities, insurance, and maintenance), food, clothing, transportation (loan repayments, insurance, license fees, gas, oil, maintenance and repairs), recreation (vacations, entertainment), medical (insurance, doctors, dentists, drugs), life insurance premiums, education, charity, and personal spending.

Now you're ready to do your own income and outgo statement. Simply make two lists—one of all your income and one of all your expenses (outgo) for the past year. If you lack good records, past income tax returns and whatever backup material you have (for example, W-2 forms, and interest or dividend statements) are often a good source of information. Once you've filled in the two lists, simply subtract total expenses from total income. Hopefully, you'll end up with more income than outgo.

Why not compile your own income and outgo statement by filling in the form in Table 2.1. Under income, list first your salary and all other earnings from your work. Then the income from investments which will include interest and dividends. Total the two sets of income figures. The outgo section covers your major expenses. These include taxes, housing, food, car, medical, savings, and so on. After each category, there's a line for the total. When both lists are completed, you are ready to do the summary.

TABLE 2.1 Income and outgo statement

Date completed _____
Date revised _____
Year _____

(a) Income

Items	Amount ($)	Remarks
Salary/wages		
Others		
Interest		
Dividends		
Others		
TOTAL INCOME	$	

(b) Outgo

Taxes		
Federal		
State and local		
Social security		
Total	$	
House		
Mortgage/rent		
Taxes		
Utilities		
Insurance		
Maintenance		
Furnishings		
Total	$	

TABLE 2.1 *(Cont.)*

Items	Amount ($)	Remarks
Food		
At home		
Dining out/take-out food		
Total	$	
Car		
Loan repayments		
Insurance/license/regis.		
Maintenance/repairs		
Running expenses		
Total	$	
Medical		
Insurance		
Doctors/Dentists		
Others		
Medication		
Total	$	
Life insurance premium		
Savings		
Retirement savings		
Charitable contributions		
Personal gifts		
Education		
Clothing		
Personal		
Miscellaneous		
TOTAL OUTGO	$	

TABLE 2.1 *(Cont.)*

<u>Summary</u>
Total income $ _____
Total outgo   − _____
  + or (−) $ _____

WHAT YOU OWN VERSUS WHAT YOU OWE

By compiling a net worth statement you will be able to see at one glance what assets you have so far acquired and what liabilities you have incurred. Hopefully, the assets column is larger than the liabilities so you'll end up with a positive net worth.

WHAT ARE ASSETS?

Broadly speaking, assets can be divided into two major categories:

1. *Liquid assets,* which can further be broken down into two groups: (1) assets that are completely liquid such as cold cash and its equivalent—checking and savings accounts as well as cash surrender value of life insurance policies, and (2) the whole spectrum of investments covering stocks, bonds, and anything else you may invest in, mutual funds, for example.

   These investments have, however, varying degrees of liquidity, which means it may take a little more time to convert them into cash. For example, as individual investors you can buy and sell stocks easier than bonds. Real estate and collectibles can also be sold for cash, but they will take longer to sell and if the timing is wrong, you may sustain huge losses.

   How much these investments are worth is based on the current market value. So, if you own 100 shares of IBM common, and they are currently trading on the New York Stock Exchange at $120 a share, then the total value of these shares is $12,000.

2. *Fixed assets* include your car, your home, and any personal belongings you may have, such as stereos, personal computers, TVs, jewelry, silverware, furniture, and clothing.

There are two ways to measure how much these are worth: replacement costs or depreciated value. Which method to use depends on the item (for example, a gold watch versus a water bed) and for what purpose. For example, the Internal Revenue Service uses fair market value, which may be significantly lower than the replacement value, that is what it will cost you to replace the item. Most insurance policies cover the actual cash value, that is, the depreciated value, unless you opt for replacement value coverage, which requires a higher premium. For antiques and other valuable items, it's a good idea to have a proper appraisal done to ensure you have the proper coverage.

WHAT ARE LIABILITIES?

Virtually anything you owe is a liability. These include:

- Taxes due to the federal, state, or local governments for income, real estate, and so on.
- Outstanding bills, which can be from charge accounts, your doctor, or anybody else to whom you owe money for goods or services performed
- Installment loans, if you borrow to buy your car, furniture, or TV, for example
- Mortgage, if you've bought a house, condo, or some other real estate

HOW TO CALCULATE YOUR NET WORTH

To calculate net worth, simply add up all your assets in one column, your liabilities in another, then subtract.

$$\text{Assets} - \text{liabilities} = \text{net worth}$$

To calculate your own net worth, use the sample format in Table 2.2.

TABLE 2.2 Your net worth

	Date completed	_____
	Date revised	_____
Year _____		

Summary

Total assets	$	_____
Total liabilities	−	_____
Net worth	$	_____

(a) What you own: your assets

Asset	Cash Value ($)
Cash	
Checking accounts	
Savings accounts	
Money market funds	
Treasury bills	
Treasury notes	
Treasury bonds	
U.S. Savings Bonds	
Stocks	
Bonds	
Mutual funds	
Tax shelter partnerships	
IRA or KEOGH	
Life insurance cash value	
Annuities	
Vested company benefits	
Deferred profit sharing	
Stock purchase plans	
Company savings plans	

TABLE 2.2 *(Cont.)*

Asset	Cash Value ($)
Accrued pension benefits	
Other	
Your house	
Your second home	
Other real estate	
Car(s)	
Boat/trailer	
Furnishings	
Electronic equipment (videos, PCs, etc.)	
Personal effects (clothing, etc.)	
Personal assets:	
Furs	
Jewelry	
Antiques	
Collections	
Hobby equipment	
Other	
What others borrowed from you	
Other	
TOTAL ASSETS:	$

TABLE 2.2 *(Cont.)*

Asset	Cash Value ($)
(b) What you owe: your liabilities	
Taxes due:	
Federal income	
State and local income	
Property	
School	
Other	
Bills pending:	
Credit cards	
Mortgage or rent	
Utilities	
Medical	
Other	
Installment loans:	
Car	
Home improvements	
Appliances	
Other	
Other loans:	
Insurance policy	
Tuition	
Broker	
Credit Card	
Other	

TABLE 2.2 *(Cont.)*

Asset	Cash Value ($)
Insurance:	
Life premiums	
Medical and disability	
Household policy	
Car	
Other	
TOTAL LIABILITIES	$

3

To Budget
or Not to Budget?

A good entrepreneur wouldn't dream of starting a business without establishing a budget. But on a personal level, most people find having a budget cramps their lifestyle. A good budget should be accurate, easy to maintain, and have a certain amount of flexibility.

Like all things financial, there's no one right way to do a budget. Much depends on your temperament and how much you like to keep track of details. It can be thorough down to the last sou or as broad as you wish, so long as it tells you accurately whether your income is sufficient to cover your expenses. You can't plan for the future if you have no idea of what's happening in the present.

A good budget tells you how you're spending your money now and whether you're doing it sensibly. It provides you with the basic information needed to plan for the future so you can allocate your resources in such a way that you'll be able to achieve your life's goals.

An *income and outgo statement* identifies the sources and uses of your resources over the last year; a *budget* is the key to how you can control your expenses. Doing a budget will help to ensure that all your expenses are accounted for and that your current income is sufficient to cover all the outgo. Knowing how you're spending your money means that you'll have a better chance of being able to balance what you earn with what you spend. In a sense, a budget is built from data you've collected on how you spent, and based on that, you can establish some guidelines for the future.

If you've never had a budget before, you may want to start by keeping a diary of your expenses. Some people do it daily—others weekly or monthly. After a few months, you'll get a feel of what works best for you. Once you have records for a year, you'll find that things don't change terribly much and you'll be able to set up a system for yourself. Be flexible. Remember: the best systems tend to be simple and easy to maintain.

ESSENTIAL AND VARIABLE EXPENSES

Expenses can be divided into two broad categories:

1. *Essential expenses* are those that you have absolutely no choice but to pay. Some of these are in fixed amounts and you know exactly how much is due and when—for example, taxes and social security, mortgage and real estate taxes or rent, car

payment, life insurance premium. To make sure you don't forget, why not include savings under this category as well? Some necessary expenses, such as utilities, telephone, food and clothing, may fluctuate in amounts from month to month.

2. *Variable expenses* is one area where you can do some meaningful planning and exert most control. For example, vacation, contributions, auto maintenance or repair, major equipment or furniture purchases such as a new couch or washer, when the old one is still usable. These are expenses that can be postponed or, if necessary, eliminated completely until a future date.

TAKING THE NEXT STEP: HOW TO GET ORGANIZED

You'll find a set of sample forms in Table 3.1 that will help you keep track of your own budget on a monthly basis.

TABLE 3.1 Keeping track monthly

Year _____

Date completed _____
Date revised _____

Summary
Total income $ ____
Total expenses $ ____
+ or (−) budget $ ____

(a) Outgo

Item ($)	Jan.	Feb.	March	April	May	June	July	Aug.	Sept.	Oct.	Nov.	Dec.	Total
Taxes													
Federal													
State/local													
Social security													
House													
Mortgage/rent													
Taxes													
Insurance													

TABLE 3.1 *(Cont.)*

Item ($)	Jan.	Feb.	March	April	May	June	July	Aug.	Sept.	Oct.	Nov.	Dec.	Total
Gas/electricity													
Telephone													
Maintenance													
Furnishings													
Food													
At home													
Dining out/ take-out food													
Car													
Loan repayment													
Insurance													
License													
Maintenance/ repairs/other													
Life insurance													

TABLE 3.1 *(Cont.)*

Item ($)	Jan.	Feb.	March	April	May	June	July	Aug.	Sept.	Oct.	Nov.	Dec.	Total
Medical													
Insurance													
Doctors/ dentists													
Medications													
Savings/ investments													
Retirement savings													
Contributions													
Gifts													
Education													
Clothing													
Personal													
Miscellaneous													
TOTAL: $													

TABLE 3.1 *(Cont.)*

Date completed _____

Date revised _____

Year _____

(b) Income

Item ($)	Jan.	Feb.	March	April	May	June	July	Aug.	Sept.	Oct.	Nov.	Dec.	Total
Salary/wages													
Commissions													
Tips													
Bonus													
Royalties													
Others													
Interest													
Dividends													
TOTAL: $													

What Are Your Major Expenses?

Major expenses tend to be ones that are compulsory and often fixed—at least to a point. Therefore, it's important to know exactly what these expenses are and what alternatives, if any, are available to you.

TAXES AND SOCIAL SECURITY

Most of us know that we need a place to live and some form of transportation to get around in, but how many of us would automatically include taxes as one of the major outgo items? Whether we want to or not, it's a fact of life that taxes eat up a good part of our income—one that you have absolutely no choice but to pay. For the average U.S. worker, taxes are a major expense item, as shown in Table 4.1, according to the Tax Foundation. In an average 8 hour day, 2 hours and 43 minutes are spent working to pay federal, state and local taxes. At this rate, the average worker worked 123 days during 1987 just to pay taxes and get to Tax Freedom Day. This is a benchmark calculated by economists at the Washington-based watchdog organization to indicate when the average taxpayer would finish fulfilling responsibilities to Federal, state, and local governments if every dollar earned from January 1 were to go exclusively to the tax collectors.

TABLE 4.1   Tax bite in the eight-hour day and tax freedom day (1980–1987)

Item	1980	1981	1982	1983	1984	1985	1986	1987
Taxes	2:39	2:43	2:41	2:38	2:36	2:38	2:39	2:43
Federal	1:48	1:52	1:48	1:43	1:42	1:44	1:44	1:46
State/local	:51	:51	:53	:54	:54	:54	:55	:57
Housing and household operation	1:24	1:23	1:30	1:29	1:31	1:27	1:28	1:27
Food/tobacco	1:03	1:01	1:04	1:03	1:04	1:00	1:00	1:00
All other	1:02	1:03	:48	:51	:46	:55	:48	:45
Transportation	:41	:40	:40	:41	:43	:41	:42	:42
Medical care	:32	:33	:37	:38	:39	:38	:39	:39
Recreation	:20	:19	:21	:21	:22	:21	:21	:21
Clothing	:19	:18	:19	:19	:19	:19	:23	:23
Tax Freedom Day	May 1	May 4	May 3	April 30	April 28	May 1	May 2	May 4

TABLE 4.1 *(Cont.)*

Notes: Figures for 1987 are forecasts. All other includes personal care, personal business, private education and research, religious and welfare activities, net foreign travel, and net savings.

Sources: Tax Foundation, derived from data supplied by the U.S. Department of Commerce, Bureau of Economic Analysis.

Since you spend a good part of your day working for Uncle Sam, it's natural you'll want to know how the Federal government spends your hard-earned dollars. Here's a breakdown, compiled by the Tax Foundation, based on a worker who earns $29,000 and is the sole source of support for a spouse and two dependent children. (See Table 4.2.) His share of the federal tax bill for fiscal 1987 totaled $7,551. This included $2,526 in income taxes, $2,074 in social security contributions and $2,951 in indirect taxes, such as his employer's share of social security taxes; corporate income taxes; excise taxes on such items as gasoline, liquor, and tobacco; and miscellaneous levies.

Where has all that money gone to?

If you feel poorer today than ten years ago, even though you're making more money—you're absolutely right. Tax Foundation calculations show that from 1977 to 1987, pretax income for the typical family rose 77% from $15,949 to $28,230, but direct federal taxes climbed by nearly 97%, from $2,399 to $4,222. Social security taxes alone more than doubled from $933 to $2,018, as increasing amounts of revenues were needed to pay for higher benefits, the result of indexing those benefits to the Consumer Price Index (CPI), and the increase in the number of beneficiaries. As a proportion of family income, direct federal taxes ranged from a low of 15% in 1977 to a high 17.2% in 1981. Since 1985, given the tax reductions, it has been marginally better— 16.7% in 1987.

Table 4.3 gives more details on median family incomes both before and after direct federal taxes and inflation. Note in particular that during the decade the CPI almost doubled, which brought the purchasing power of each dollar down to 53 cents, as measured in 1977 dollars. Rising prices combined with a rising tax bite have dropped the family's purchasing power nearly 8% in the last ten years.

TABLE 4.2   How the federal government spent a worker's tax
dollars in fiscal 1987

Function	Worker's Share		Total Spending (millions $)
	Amount ($)	Percent of total (%)	
Income security	2,387	31.61	332,770
National defense	2,024	26.81	282,246
Net interest	986	13.06	137,461
Health	798	10.57	111,279
Agriculture	223	2.95	31,084
Education, training, social services, and employment	214	2.83	29,808
Transportation	194	2.57	27,017
Veterans' benefits and services	191	2.53	26,679
International affairs	105	1.39	14,607
Natural resources and environment	100	1.32	13,857
General science, space, and technology	68	.90	9,523
Commerce and housing credit	66	.88	9,300
Administration of justice	60	.79	8,293
General government	49	.65	6,840
Community and regional development	44	.59	6,167
Energy	27	.36	3,787
General purpose fiscal assistance	14	.18	1,944
TOTAL	7,551	100.00	1,015,572

Notes: Income security includes social security, federal employee retirement, unemployment compensation, housing assistance, food and nutrition assistance; excludes veterans' income security. Health includes medicare, medicaid, and others; and excludes veterans' hospital and medical care.

A major federal spending is payments for individuals, which in 1987 added up to $465.3 billion, a cost of $3,338 for the moderate-income family, or 44 cents of every tax dollar. This covers the income security and health items in the table, as well as payments for veterans, assistance to students, and other payments to individuals under special programs.

Sources: Tax Foundation computations, based on Federal Budget presented January 5, 1987 (Office of Management and Budget) and tax laws from the Treasury Department.

A closer look at the last ten years shows that this decrease has been quite neatly divided in half. During the first four years, between 1977 and 1981, inflation and rising federal taxes slashed 13% from this median family's purchasing power. It was a period when increases in

TABLE 4.3 Median family incomes before and after direct federal taxes and inflation (1977–1987)

Year	Median Family Income ($)	Direct Federal Taxes			After-Tax Income	
		Income tax ($)	Social security ($)	Total ($)	Current dollars	1987 dollars
1977	15,949	1,466	933	2,399	13,550	25,518
1978	17,318	1,717	1,048	2,765	14,553	25,442
1979	19,048	1,881	1,168	3,049	15,999	25,116
1980	20,586	2,143	1,262	3,405	17,181	23,763
1981	21,462	2,267	1,427	3,694	17,768	22,266
1982	23,036	2,342	1,543	3,885	19,151	22,610
1983	23,943	2,277	1,604	3,881	20,062	22,954
1984	25,415	2,395	1,703	4,098	21,317	23,374
1985	25,992	2,466	1,832	4,298	21,694	23,005
1986	27,144	2,865	1,941	4,806	22,338	23,220
1987	28,230	2,704	2,018	4,722	23,508	23,508

Notes: Median income is for all families with one earner employed full time, year round. Income tax based on married couple filing jointly with two dependent children. 1987 dollars adjusted by CPI of the Bureau of Labor Statistics; assumes 4% inflation in 1987. Figures for 1987 are estimates by the Tax Foundation.

Sources: Tax Foundation computations based on data from the U.S. Department of Commerce, Bureau of the Census; U.S. Department of Labor, Bureau of Labor Statistics; and the Treasury Department, Internal Revenue Service.

federal income and social security taxes averaged over 10% a year. Inflation was also climbing at a comparable, double-digit rate. The worker's pretax nominal income, however, was increasing by only 8% a year.

Since 1981, however, although this family's nominal income has increased an average of just under 5% a year, its purchasing power has risen at almost a 0.9% rate. The reason: the hold on inflation and income taxes is working in the family's favor. Thanks to the Economic Recovery Tax Act of 1981, federal direct taxes have risen by only 4% a year; consumer prices, too, have been tamed, going up by an average of less than 4% a year. However, the social security tax continues to grow unabated and still outpaces the gains in the paycheck.

Post-tax reform

At this point, you may say, wait, how about tax reform? Won't I be paying less taxes from now on? Like everything about taxes, that depends. Let's see why.

All that talk about tax simplification and reform in the mid-1980s finally resulted in the momentous Tax Reform Act of 1986. Since tax reform changes many of the most basic rules, it will have a far-reaching impact, touching the lives of everyone. Most provisions were effective as of January 1987, but many others will be phased in gradually. What this means is that at certain higher income levels—say, household income of about $75,000 and up—you may end up paying more taxes during the transition year, that is 1987, when the lower rates were phased in, but the deductions you were accustomed to claiming were repealed by tax reform. Also, your personal status (whether single, head of household, or married) as well as where you reside may make a difference as to how tax reform affects you.

Following is a brief summary of the major changes that affect all taxpayers under tax reform. Changes that pertain to specific situations will be discussed later on in this chapter as well as in other appropriate spots throughout this book.

- Cuts in tax rates and brackets.   U.S. income taxes are based on a graduated tax-rate system. That means, the higher your income, the more taxes you'll pay. For individuals, the major provision in tax reform is to cut sharply the top tax rate from 50% to 28%. At the same time, the number of tax brackets will be reduced to just 2 from 14 by 1988. Joint filers pay 15% on taxable income under $29,750; 28% above that. For singles, the cutoff is $17,850.

So far, it sounds simple enough. In practice, there is more than that. At certain income levels, you may incur one or possibly two rate surcharges. For example, an additional 5% surcharge would apply to some portion of high incomes, beginning at $71,900, for joint filers, and $43,150 for singles. What this means is, if you earn $100,000 and file a joint return, everything up to $71,900 will be taxed at 28%. The remaining $28,100 will incur the 5% surcharge and be taxed at 33%.

For the 1987 tax return that you file, there will be five tax rates, ranging from 11% to 38.5%.

- Return of the standard deduction.   Now that you've just gotten used to the term *zero bracket amount*, Congress has changed it once again back to the standard deduction. Taxpayers who do not itemize will get a big bonus from the higher standard deduction provided by the Tax Reform Act of 1986. Also, an increasing number of taxpayers who used to itemize may find it is to their advantage *not* to itemize and thus simplify their tax-filing.

  As with the tax bracket reduction, the increased standard deduction will be effective in 1988. This means in 1989, when it's time to file those 1988 returns, couples filing jointly will get a standard deduction of $5,000, increased from $3,670 for 1986; heads of household will get $4,400; and singles will get $3,000, instead of the current $2,480.

  Note: For 1987, the standard deduction will be the same as 1986, with an adjustment to account for inflation. After 1988, the deduction will continue to be adjusted each year for inflation.

- Changes in the personal exemption.   Along with the rise in the standard deduction, tax reform also increases the personal exemption. This double treat would sharply reduce taxes for most low-income taxpayers, particularly those with large families.

  The personal exemption will go up in steps, rising to

$1,900 for 1987, $1,950 for 1988 and $2,000 for 1989, from $1,080 for 1986. Beginning in 1990, the exemption would be adjusted annually for inflation.

Starting in 1988—that is, for returns filed in 1989—the benefit of the personal exemption is phased out for higher-income taxpayers whose taxable income exceeds $149,250 for joint filers, $123,790 for heads of household, and $89,560 for singles. This is done by applying a 5% surtax on taxable income until the tax benefit of each exemption has been eliminated. Also beginning in 1988, the additional personal exemptions for the elderly and blind will be repealed.

● Comply or . . . .   Be warned now: post tax reform, the IRS will act much as banks have been doing in recent years, with your savings receiving a much lower rate than you are paying on some loans. The Tax Reform Act of 1986 contains a number of compliance provisions. One provision would allow the IRS to pay a lower rate of interest on refunds—8% during the first two quarters in 1987—than what you'd have to pay them, 9%, if you owed them back taxes.

The penalty for failure to pay tax when due, has also been increased to one percent a month from one half of one percent. Also changed is the date when the penalty starts ticking. Post-tax reform, the interest on the penalty starts from the due date of the income tax return, not from the time the IRS makes a demand. Between the interest and the increased penalty, plus the nondeductibility of consumer interest, it can get costly for a taxpayer who wants to take an aggressive stand with the IRS.

Post-tax reform, it will get even more expensive if you substantially understate your tax liabilities. The penalty for this offense is being increased to at least 20% from 10%. Note, the IRS has yet to issue a clarification on whether the increase is 20%, according to the Tax Reform Act, or 25%, as based on the Omnibus Budget Reconcilation Act—two pieces of legislation signed by President Reagan on successive days.

If you are self-employed and file quarterly payments of estimated tax, take special notice that such payments must now total 90%, up from 80%, of the total tax liability for the year. Exempt from this rule are those whose final bill exceeds withheld taxes by less than $500 or who did not owe any tax for the previous year. As we enter the tax reform era, one way not to be caught short is to do better budgeting for taxes.

Keeping track

For most taxpayer–houseowners, it's estimated that about one third of gross income goes towards paying taxes of all types, including social security. With tax reform drastically reducing the number of deductions that you can claim, it is all the more important to keep good records so each year when tax-filing time rolls along, you'll be able to take the utmost advantage of whatever is still available. Good records are also important in the event you're audited; the Internal Revenue Service will generally disallow deductions that cannot be adequately substantiated.

Because there's no specific requirement that records be kept in any particular way, it's up to you to devise your own system. The trick here is to know exactly the type of information that you should collect. What works best is one that's simple and easy to keep up to date.

The first step is to set up a filing system where you can park your bills and receipts. Label a folder or envelope for each deduction or other topics on which you expect paperwork. As these come in, file them immediately. For some items like out-of-pocket expenses for volunteer work or business entertainment, you should also keep a diary answering in detail the questions when, how much, where, who, and why. When it's time to do some tax-planning or to file your tax returns again, you'll have all the necessary data at your fingertips.

Start now and use the forms in Tables 4.4 through 4.7 to set up your own tax records.

Know your tax bracket

To calculate your tax bracket, you'll need to have some idea what your income will be, as well as the number of exemptions and types of deductions that you'll be entitled to claim. If you have past tax returns, it may help to have them in front of you as you try to figure out your current bracket. The forms in Tables 4.8 through 4.10 take you through the long 1040 tax form and schedule A, where you can claim most of the itemized deductions. Table 4.8 is divided into three columns so you can have in one place the actual numbers for 1986, the last year before tax

TABLE 4.4 Car log

| Date | Client and Purpose | Odometer Reading | | | Tolls/ Parking |
		Begin	End	Total miles	

TABLE 4.5 Personal computer usage log

| Date | User and Purpose | Time | | | Supplies Purchased |
		Begin	End	Total	

TABLE 4.6 Entertainment log

Date	Guests Entertained and Purpose	Expense Description Place and Nature	Amount

TABLE 4.7   Volunteer work expense log

Date	Organization	Purpose	Amount

reform took hold, the actual numbers for 1987, if you're lucky enough to have filed your tax return already, and your estimates for 1988. With Congress in search of ways to reduce the federal deficit, it is quite possible that they may eventually decide to take back some of those reductions.

TABLE 4.8   Your tax bracket at a glance

Item	1986	1987	1988
Income			
1. Wages/salaries/ bonus	$_____	$_____	$_____
2. Interest income	_____	_____	_____
3. Dividends	_____	_____	_____
4. Tax refunds from state	_____	_____	_____
5. Alimony received	_____	_____	_____
6. Business income/ loss	_____	_____	_____
7. Net capital gains	_____	_____	_____
8. Partnership income/loss	_____	_____ *	_____ *
9. Other income	_____	_____	_____
10. Total income (add items 1 to 9)	_____	_____	_____
Adjustments to income			
11. Employee moving expenses	[_____]	[___0___]	[___0___]
12. Employee business expenses	[_____]	[___0___]	[___0___]
13. Miscellaneous	[___0___]	[_____]	[_____]
14. IRA deduction: $2,000; with nonworking spouse, $2,250	[_____]	[_____]	[adjustment $2,000 each]
15. Keogh deduction	[_____]	[_____]	[_____]
16. Alimony paid	[_____]	[_____]	[_____]
17. Two-earner marriage deduction	[_____]	[___0___]	[___0___]
18. Child/dependent care deduction	[___0___]	[_____]	[_____]
19. Total adjustments (add items 11 to 18)	[_____]	[_____]	[_____]

TABLE 4.8 *(Cont.)*

Item	1986	1987	1988
20. Adjusted gross income (AGI) (item 10 less item 19)			
Itemized deductions			
21. Medical expenses in excess of 7½% of AGI in 1987 and 1988			
22. State and local income and real estate taxes			
23. Other taxes (including sales taxes)		0	0
24. Housing mortgage interest			
25. All other interest		*	*
26. Employee moving expenses	0		
27. Charitable contributions			
28. Casualty losses in excess of 10% of AGI			
29. Miscellaneous in excess of 2% of AGI			
30. Subtotal deductions (add items 21 to 29)			
31. Less $3,540 for joint; $2,390 if single		0	0
32. Net deductions (Subtract item 30 from item 31; itemize only if item 30 is larger than 31)			
33. Plus exemptions for each dependent take this amount . . . ($2,000 for 1989)	$1,080	$1,900	$1,950

TABLE 4.8 *(Cont.)*

Item	1986	1987	1988
34. Total deductions and exemptions (add items 32 and 33)	_____	_____	_____

*Passive losses and consumer interest subject to phaseout. For details see section *What are credits and deductions?*

Tax basics

Familiarizing yourself with some of the tax basics will help make tax filing—not to mention planning—an easier task to handle, and may just possibly help to save you a few hard-earned dollars.

What forms to use. You need to file a federal income tax return only if your gross income is in excess of $3,560, if single ($4,640 or more, if 65 or older), and $5,830, if married filing jointly ($6,910 if either of the joint filers is 65 or older, and $7,990 if both are 65 or older). You should also file a return if you want to claim a refund.

What tax form you use may make a difference. You have three choices

1. 1040EZ
2. 1040 short form
3. 1040 long form

As the title implies, the 1040EZ is easy to use. There are only 11 steps. But not everyone can use it. You must be single, with no dependents, have a taxable income under $50,000, and receive most of it from salary or wages.

The short form, 1040A, is roughly twice as long as the EZ, but it's more flexible. You can be married or single, and have dividend or interest income of any amount.

If your taxable income is over $50,000, you must file the long

TABLE 4.9   1987 tax rates at a glance

Married Filing Jointly and Qualifying Widows/ Widowers, Taxable Income, ($)	Rate (%)	Married Filing Separately, Taxable Income, ($)
0 to 3,000	11	0 to 1,500
3,000 to 28,000	15	1,500 to 14,000
28,000 to 45,000	28	14,000 to 22,500
45,000 to 90,000	35	22,500 to 45,000
Over 90,000	38.5	Over 45,000

Heads of Household, Taxable Income, ($)	Rate (%)	Singles, Taxable Income, ($)
0 to 2,500	11	0 to 1,800
2,500 to 23,000	15	1,800 to 16,800
23,000 to 38,000	28	16,800 to 27,000
38,000 to 80,000	35	27,000 to 54,000
Over 80,000	38.5	Over 54,000

TABLE 4.10   1988 tax rates at a glance

Married Filing Jointly and Qualifying Widows/ Widowers, Taxable Income, ($)	Rate (%)	Married Filing Separately, Taxable Income, ($)
0 to 29,750	15	0 to 17,850
29,750 to 71,900	28	17,850 to 43,150
71,900 to 149,250	33	43,150 to 89,560
Over 149,250	33/28*	Over 89,560

Heads of Household, Taxable Income, ($)	Rate (%)	Singles, Taxable Income, ($)
0 to 29,750	15	0 to 17,850
29,750 to 71,900	28	17,850 to 43,150
71,900 to 149,250	33	43,150 to 89,560
Over 149,250	33/28*	Over 89,560

*Surtax bracket continues until personal exemptions are used up.

form. On the other hand, if your taxable income is less than that, but you have a large number of deductions and credits to claim (more on those in the following pages) and want to take advantage of them, you should use the long form.

If you won the lottery jackpot last year or made some money in the stock market, you must file the long form. If you had income from a taxable pension, annuity, rents, royalties or partnerships, the long form is also for you.

If your parents claim you as a dependent on their return, but you had interest, dividends, or other unearned income of $1,080 or more, then you must also file the long form.

Filing certain forms also requires you to use the 1040. For instance, when you apply for extension of time to file, or if you sell or exchange your principal residence, you'll need to use the 1040.

What if you have a choice between the long or short form? Try it both ways and see which one gives you the best break.

To itemize or not.   The federal tax law gives each individual taxpayer a standard deduction. Prior to tax reform, this was called the *zero bracket amount*. This amount varies depending on your filing status.

For 1987, married persons filing jointly will get $3,760; if filing separately, the deduction will be $1,880; singles or heads of household, $2,540. For 1988, the standard deduction increases to $5,000 for joint filers; $2,500 for married filing separately; $4,400 for heads of household and $3,000 for singles. Starting in 1989, the standard deduction will be indexed for inflation.

Generally, it's more advantageous for married couples to file jointly—even though tax reform has repealed the two-earner deduction. This entitled couples who both earned income to take a 10% deduction of the lower earned income up to a maximum of $30,000 or a maximum deduction of $3,000.

Whether you should itemize or not depends on how much you've spent for items such as medical and dental expenses, state and local taxes, interests, contributions, casualty and theft losses, and miscellaneous. If the total exceeds your allowable standard deduction, then you should itemize. If not, start doing some 1988 tax planning now so you can itemize next time. By bunching your deductions, you can itemize one year and take the standard amount the next.

What is income?   Everyone knows that salaries, wages, commissions, and tips are income. But do you know that alimony, bonuses, embezzlement proceeds, gambling winnings, jury fees, kickbacks, and rewards are also income? Some employer-paid expenses are also considered income—for example, financial counselling fees, health resort expenses, and employer scholarship plans that benefit an employee's child.

How to get from gross to taxable income.   When you file the 1040 long form, the first thing you'll have to do is to calculate your total or gross income. This includes all taxable income such as:

- wages
- salaries
- tips
- commissions
- bonuses
- dividends
- alimony
- annuities
- pensions
- gains from sales or exchanges
- state and local income tax refunds
- rents

After adding these up, subtract certain items, known as adjustments, such as:

- alimony payments
- IRA or Keogh contributions
- losses from sales or exchanges (limited to $3,000)

The result is your adjusted gross income (AGI).

Subtract the excess itemized deductions from your AGI. That is the result of total itemized deductions minus your standard deduction. The final step: deduct the number of exemptions, which is $1900 for 1987, $1950 for 1988, and $2000 for 1989 for each dependent you're claiming, including yourself, and you'll end up with your taxable income.

What are credits and deductions?   Credits are worth a lot more than deductions because they reduce your taxes dollar-for-dollar, so it's worthwhile to seek out all the credits you can claim. Although tax reform has repealed the political contributions and investment tax credits, there are still others available that you can claim if you qualify.

For example, tax reform gives low-income families with children a special break by substantially expanding the earned income credit. For 1987, the refundable earned income credit will increase to 14% of the first $5,714 of earned income, from 11% of $5,000, or a maximum credit of $800 versus $550. The credit would be phased out for workers earning between $9,000 and $17,000. To claim this credit, you must file a tax return, even if no taxes are deducted from wages, or if income earned is not enough to file one. You may get an advance payment of the credit through reduced withholding by filing a W-5 form with your employer, stating eligibility to claim it and that no other form is on file with another employer.

Tax reform left intact the child and dependent care credit, which can be claimed on Form 2441. This entitles you to deduct a part of the expenses you incur to care for a dependent child or relative so you can go to work. The amount of credit you may deduct is based on income. If, for example, your 1987 adjusted gross income is $10,000 or less, you can claim a credit equal to 30% of employment-related expenses, up to a maximum of $720 for one child and $1,440 for two or more. But the credit declines as your income rises. For incomes of $28,000 or more, the credit is limited to 20% of the amount spent for such care, or a maximum of $480 for one child and $960 for two or more.

For details on the elderly credit please turn to the next section, *Autumn and Winter.*

Deductions, on the other hand, cut taxes at best at the highest tax rate imposed on your adjusted gross income. This means that the higher your income, the more your deduction is worth. If you're in the 28% tax bracket, for every dollar of deduction, you'll save 28 cents. But if you're in the 15% tax bracket, each deducted dollar is worth only 15 cents.

There are two types of deductions: (1) those from gross income, such as alimony payments, disability income exclusion, or contributions to IRAs or Keogh plans, and (2) those from adjusted gross income, the itemized deductions, claimed mostly on Schedule A, such as medical expenses, interest, property taxes, or state and local income taxes. As some of the biggest savings used to come from these itemized deductions, this was one area where tax reform tried to make the biggest dents. The result: taxpayers who itemize will no longer be able to take advantage of certain long-standing deductions.

For example, the deduction for state and local sales tax would be eliminated. Limited partnership losses and consumer interest deductions, such as those for interest paid on credit cards or car loans, would be phased out over five years. For 1987, you will be able to deduct only 65% of such consumer interest—so if you have paid $100 in interest expenses, you'll be able to deduct only $65. For 1988, you will be able to deduct 40%, in 1989, 20%, in 1990, 10%, and in 1991, nothing at all. Note, in particular, the new rule will also apply to interest you pay on life insurance policy loans, or to the IRS on taxes you owe. So, if you owe the federal government back taxes and interest, this is a good time to think about paying up so you can take at least a portion of the deduction this year.

Still deductible, but now limited to the extent of your investment income, are the interest expenses incurred in your investing activities such as trading on margin, for example. Let's say you have incurred $6,000 in interest expenses but your investment income, which includes dividends, interest, and capital gains, totaled only $5,000. Your deduction would be $5,000.

Also harder to deduct are medical and miscellaneous expenses. As of 1987, the floor under the medical deduction is increased to 7.5% from 5% of adjusted gross income. If your AGI is $25,000 your medical expenses would have to exceed $1,875 before you could start deducting.

If you itemized prior to tax reform, you could take a variety of job-related expenses—such as uniforms, dues to unions or professional associations, and business journals—and deduct them under an umbrella label called *miscellaneous*. With tax reform, it will be harder to do so. Now, you must first meet a 2% floor of AGI. If your AGI is $40,000, your miscellaneous expenses will have to be in excess of $800 before you can start deducting.

For homeowners, there is good news. Tax reform left virtually intact the mortgage interest deduction. The interest you incur to finance a mortgage on a first home—or even a second home for that matter—would still be completely deductible, as long as it doesn't exceed the purchase price of the home plus the cost of any improvements. Note, this limit rule applies only to home mortgage loans taken out after August 17, 1986.

Now that consumer interest is an endangered species, a home equity loan seems extra attractive since the interest on it is still deductible. The proceeds, however, must be used for home purchase or improvement, although medical or education expenses will also qualify. In recent months, many banks and thrifts have been promoting home equity loans as an easy source for cash. As your home will be used as the collateral, make sure you know exactly what is involved. Check, in particular, the extra fees and points that you may incur, as well as how high the rates may go, if interest rates were to trend upward once again.

For more details about home equity loans, see the section entitled *Using your home as a bank* later in this chapter.

If you do not itemize, 1986 was the last year that you could deduct for a charitable contribution. For those who itemize, the charitable contribution deduction would still be available.

Fire, theft, or other casualty losses caused by some sudden unexpected event—vandalism, frost damage, or sonic boom—will still qualify for some tax relief if you meet two requirements. These are a $100 deductible and a floor of 10% of adjusted gross income.

For example, say your AGI is $35,000. During the year, you sustained a $2,000 casualty loss, none of which is insured. First you have to deduct $100. Then take 10% of the remaining $1,900, which is $190. Subtract this $190 from $1,900 and you come up with $1,710, the amount that you will be allowed to deduct as a casualty loss.

Although tax reform repealed the deduction for state sales taxes, it left intact the deductions for the other taxes, such as state and local income, real estate, and personal property. For taxpayers who live in high-tax states, such as New York and California, the savings from these deductions can be substantial.

If you itemize, you'll be interested in comparing your own deductions with Table 4.11, which shows the average deductions of taxpayers before tax reform for interest, taxes, charitable contributions, and medical expenses. Obviously when tax reform becomes completely effective, these averages will probably look quite different. For one, many in the lower income groups may no longer be able to meet the new requirements for some of the deductions, such as medical expenses, and may opt instead for the higher standard deduction provided by tax reform rather than itemizing.

TABLE 4.11 Average itemized deductions for 1985 based on preliminary IRS information

Adjusted Gross Income Ranges ($)	Average Deductions			
	Medical ($)	Taxes ($)	Contributions ($)	Interest ($)
Under $5,000	3,165	640	438	3,425
5,000 under 10,000	3,118	1,094	607	2,528
10,000 under 15,000	2,393	1,259	787	2,757
15,000 under 20,000	1,862	1,579	819	2,839
20,000 under 25,000	1,713	1,830	809	3,220
25,000 under 30,000	1,379	2,133	800	3,591
30,000 under 40,000	1,639	2,696	891	4,121
40,000 under 50,000	1,727	3,483	1,105	5,234
50,000 under 75,000	2,799	4,750	1,575	6,730
75,000 under 100,000	5,550	6,942	2,538	10,038
100,000 under 200,000	8,500	11,034	4,237	14,419
200,000 under 500,000	27,592	24,407	15,014	23,473
500,000 under 1,000,000	43,258	55,646	45,696	43,705
1,000,000 and more	58,435	162,463	140,071	100,620

Source: Reproduced with permission from *Federal Tax Guide Reports.* Published and copyrighted by Commerce Clearing House, Inc., 4025 N. Peterson Ave., Chicago, IL, 60646.

Tax tips for varying seasons

Spring

If you're a student working part time or only during summer vacations, you may not earn enough money to have to pay income tax. By claiming the exemption from withholding on the W-4 form with your employer, you will have more money in your pocket sooner, and it will also save you the trouble of having to file an income tax return to claim the refund.

Summer

Tax reform will eliminate the practice of transferring income to young children to avoid taxes. After October 22, 1986, all unearned income in excess of $1,000 of a child under 14 years old generally would be taxed at the parents' top marginal rate.

For example, say, your child has unearned income of $1,300. Of this, he is entitled to a standard deduction of $500, plus another $500 to be taxed at his own rate. The remaining $300, or net unearned income, will be taxed at your top rate.

Net unearned income is calculated as follows: unearned income less the sum of $500 and the greater of (1) $500 of the standard deduction or $500 of itemized deductions, or (2) the amount of allowable deductions that are directly connected with the production of the unearned income.

Tax reform also eliminated Clifford trusts, which previously were used to reduce taxes on assets transferred to children. This was done on the assumption that the child paid a lower tax rate than the parents. So during the ten years that such trusts had to be in effect, the income was taxed at the child's rate. After that period, the capital was returned to the parents.

If you can claim your children as dependents on your tax return, then they will no longer be able to claim the personal exemption on their own returns. Under previous law, the exemption could often be claimed on both tax returns. Finally, the act has a provision designed to stop taxpayers from claiming nonexistent dependents, and to discourage both divorced parents from claiming the same child as a dependent. For each person over five years old that you claim as a dependent, you must now include on your tax return a taxpayer identification number—generally a social security number.

Autumn and winter

Before tax reform, if you were 65 or older, you were entitled to two, and possibly three, exemptions. In 1987—that is, for returns to be filed in 1988—these extra exemptions are replaced by one, and possibly two, standard deductions. For married couples, this deduction is $600 (double that amount to $1,200 if both elderly and blind); for single people, the amount is $750 ($1,500, if both elderly and blind).

In addition, you'll be given an extra break by having the higher standard deduction a year earlier than the rest of the population. For 1987, you will get the increased standard deduction amounts generally applicable for 1988—that is, $5,000 for married individuals filing jointly, $4,400 for heads of household, and $3,000 for single taxpayers.

Unchanged is the elderly credit, designed to assist taxpayers who receive small amounts of social security, railroad retirement and other pension, annuity or disability benefits, and have relatively small amounts of other income. If you're 65 or older, or simply retired and disabled, you may be able to claim it. If you're single, the credit is based on 15% of the first $5,000 of annual income of any type, or a maximum of $750. If married filing jointly, and both you and your spouse are over 65, you can claim 15% of up to $7,500, or $1,125.

If you're 55 or older, you may exclude from your gross income $125,000 of gain on the sale of your home. Just remember: to qualify for this one-time exclusion, you must reach 55 by the date you sell the home. See chapter 9 for more tax tips for older taxpayers.

All seasons

Filing a new W-4.   The extra dollars you've been seeing in your paycheck lately may not be yours after all. The reason: because of the sweeping changes brought on by tax reform, the amount of taxes being withheld may not be sufficient to cover your tax liabilities. While the withholding calculations are geared to the new law's lower rates and larger exemptions, the number of allowances claimed is based on the old law, which contained many deductions and credits that are no longer available. For 1987, each allowance claimed reduces income subject to withholding by $1,900, up from $1,080 in 1986.

To ensure the correct amount is being withheld, the Tax Reform Act of 1986 required that you complete a new withholding allowance certificate, Form W-4, before October 1, 1987. It's advisable to review your W-4 form periodically. Otherwise, you may find at year's end, you've been significantly underwithheld and might be subject to costly penalties, plus interest on overdue amounts, if withholdings—plus quarterly estimated tax payments, if any—don't equal at least 90% of the year's liability, or 100% of the previous year's liability. You may also incur additional penalties, if an underpayment is deemed to be due to negligence or fraud (see the section entitled *Post-tax reform* for more details on interest rates and penalties).

Instead of simplifying the process, the new W-4 form complicated the process. In fact, the new form received such bad reviews the IRS had to issue a revision.

If your tax situation is a simple one, you need complete only five lines of the worksheet to figure the number of allowances you should claim. If, however, you itemize, then you will have to tackle a few more issues. Here are some tips to keep in mind

- If both you and your spouse work, you should sit down together and figure out the total number of exemptions you should claim. Let the spouse with the higher income claim all the withholding exemptions.
- Claim all the withholding allowances to which you are entitled if you want to balance the amount of tax withheld with what's owed at year end.
- You can always claim fewer allowances than you are entitled to but not more.
- Although there's no limit to the number of withholding allowances that you may claim, as long as they can be supported, note that if you claim more than 10, down from 14 before tax reform, your employer is required to submit a copy of the W-4 to the IRS for possible review.

Capital gains.   For investors, the major change in the tax reform bill is the elimination of preferential treatment for long-term capital gains. Under prior law, you incurred a top rate of 20% on the appreciation of assets such as common stock, gold, stamps, and coins if they were sold after being held at least six months. The gains on items held for less time were treated as ordinary income, taxable at up to 50%. With tax reform, both short- and long-term gains will be taxed at the uniform top rate of 28%. Note, even though the highest tax bracket for 1987 will be 38.5%, there is a separate clause in the act limiting the capital gains tax to 28%. The most obvious impact of this change could be to increase trading, resulting in more business for brokers of all types.

Experts say that with a 28% tax on all capital gains investors will now place more emphasis on income and less on capital gains. Investors will be less willing to put their money into stocks that are considered risky because there would essentially be less reward in such chancy securities. Highly volatile issues, such as technology stocks and a wide array of emerging growth stocks, fared poorly in this climate, at least initially. Instead, investors are moving into stocks that pay high dividends and carry less risk such as telephone and electric utilities. Some investors may forgo common stocks completely and go into high-yielding bonds.

Alternative minimum tax.   If you have made abundant use of tax breaks to cut your tax bills in the past, tax reform will now make it harder for you to do so. The alternative minimum tax is Congress' way of making sure that everyone pays some taxes. If your tax liability is greater under minimum tax than regular, then you must take the alternative route.

This is how it works: to calculate the minimum tax, you'll take your taxable income and add back certain tax preferences, such as percentage depletion, accelerated depreciation, and intangible drilling costs. With tax reform, you'll also have to include certain interest paid on newly issued tax-exempt bonds for so-called nonessential functions, and all passive losses from tax shelters and other investments in which the investor doesn't actively participate. Joint filers then could exempt $40,000 of that amount; single filers, $30,000. A tax of 21% would be paid on the remaining amount.

The exemption amounts would be phased out for high-income taxpayers, who would end up paying approximately a 26% rate. For amounts that exceed $150,000 for joint filers—$112,500 for singles—the minimum tax will claim 25 cents of every dollar.

Tax shelters.   Under tax reform, you will no longer be able to use paper losses generated by tax shelters to reduce tax liability. This means "passive losses" from limited partnerships, or any other businesses, in which you do not materially participate, cannot be used to offset income from other sources such as salary or portfolio income. The only way now is to use such losses to offset income from similar passive investments.

This loss-limitation rule will also be applied to all rental income, which includes but is not limited to real estate, regardless of whether you participate in managing the property or not. But there is an exception: if your AGI is under $100,000, you are allowed to use up to $25,000 of losses on rental real estate. If your AGI exceeds $100,000, then the allowance would be reduced by 50% of the amount by which income exceeds the hundred grand. For example, an AGI of $150,000 would be allowed as much as $25,000 in rental real estate losses.

As with the consumer interest rule, this tax-shelter provision is to be phased in over five years to make the changes less traumatic. You can deduct 65% of losses for 1987, 40% for 1988, 20% for 1989, 10% for 1990, and none at all by 1991.

Business investments.   The Tax Reform Act of 1986 repealed the investment tax credit, retroactively for any property placed in service after January 1, 1986. This means equipment such as computers, copiers, typewriters, chairs, and desks that are bought for business use will no longer qualify for the 6% to 10% tax credit.

Tax reform also reduced depreciation allowances somewhat. For example, automobiles and light trucks will be written off over five years, instead of three years as under previous laws. Most types of manufacturing equipment will be written off over seven years, rather than five years.

If you own apartments or houses that you rent out, you'll have to depreciate them over 27.5 years rather than 19 years.

If you entertain a great deal in your business, the expenses you'll incur will be worth much less under tax reform. The cost of meals and entertainment, previously fully deductible, is now only 80% deductible.

SHELTER

To buy or to rent?

Most people opt for buying if they can even though renting is still generally a cheaper option—at least on a purely cash-flow basis (see Table 4.14)—despite the recent downward trend in mortgage interest rates. The argument for buying includes tax benefits—tax reform left intact the deduction for mortgage interest and real estate taxes—and the hope to reap sizable gains when it's time to sell. As you can see in Table 4.12, when inflation rates climbed (1973 to 1981), house prices

TABLE 4.12 House prices compared with median family income plus the average interest rates and annual family income required (1968–1986)

Year	House Price ($)	House Percent change	Interest (%)	Income Required ($)	Median Family Income ($)	Median Family Percent change	Inflation Annual Rate (%)
1968	20,100		7.03	N.A.	8,632		+ 4.2
1969	21,800	+ 8.5	7.82	N.A.	9,433	+ 9.3	+ 5.4
1970	23,000	+ 5.5	8.35	N.A.	9,867	+ 4.6	+ 5.9
1971	24,800	+ 7.8	7.67	N.A.	10,285	+ 4.2	+ 4.3
1972	26,700	+ 7.7	7.52	N.A.	11,116	+ 8.1	+ 3.3
1973	28,900	+ 8.2	8.01	N.A.	12,051	+ 8.4	+ 6.2
1974	32,000	+ 10.7	9.02	N.A.	12,902	+ 7.1	+ 11.0
1975	35,300	+ 10.3	9.21	N.A.	13,719	+ 6.3	+ 9.1
1976	38,100	+ 7.9	9.11	N.A.	14,958	+ 9.0	+ 5.8
1977	42,900	+ 12.6	9.02	N.A.	16,010	+ 7.0	+ 6.5
1978	48,700	+ 13.5	9.58	N.A.	17,640	+ 9.2	+ 7.7
1979	55,700	+ 14.4	10.92	N.A.	19,680	+ 11.6	+ 11.3
1980	62,200	+ 11.7	12.95	26,122	21,020	+ 6.8	+ 13.5
1981	66,400	+ 6.7	15.12	32,485	22,388	+ 6.5	+ 10.4
1982	67,800	+ 2.1	15.38	26,430	23,433	+ 4.7	+ 6.1
1983	70,300	+ 3.7	12.85	23,988	24,580	+ 4.9	+ 3.2
1984	72,400	+ 3.0	12.49	24,240	26,433	+ 7.5	+ 4.3
1985	75,500	+ 4.3	11.74	29,243	27,940	+ 4.7	+ 3.8
1986	80,600	+ 6.8	10.25	27,631	29,200	+ 4.5	+ 1.1

Notes: Median prices for existing houses. N.A. = Not available.
Source: National Association of Realtors, Washington, D.C.

kept pace and pulled ahead. A home or a piece of investment real estate proved to be a good inflation hedge. More recently, home prices have been rising almost on a par with inflation.

How much house can you afford?

What you want in a house may be quite different from what you really need. But the more crucial question is: How much house can you afford? One commonly used rule of thumb says you shouldn't pay more than 2½ times your gross income. So if you earn $20,000, you can afford a $50,000 house. But can you really afford even that much? The high costs of the utilities and maintenance you'll need to pay are not included in this figure.

The second rule of thumb says to spend no more than 30% of your gross income for housing. By this, you'll have to figure what your monthly budget should be based on your income. For instance, if you earn $2,000 a month, $600 will be the maximum you can spend on housing, including all operating and maintenance costs. Obviously, neither rule is perfect. There are other considerations as well: your lifestyle, whether you have a steady or a sporadic income, the size of your downpayment, the amount of money you'll borrow and at what interest rate. All these will play a part as well.

Just remember though—what a lender permits you to borrow may differ greatly from what you can in reality afford. The lenders need to worry only about what you owe them. But you have to consider a multitude of other expenses, of which housing is only one.

Who is a home buyer?

Today's home buyer is older and must have a higher income than those back in 1983, says the United States League of Savings Institutions' 1985 home buyer survey. According to this study, *Home-ownership/Returning to Tradition*, roughly half of all home-buying households in 1985 had to have a second earner to meet this higher income requirement. Table 4.13 provides details on the profile of a home buyer in the recent past.

TABLE 4.13   Who is a home buyer?

	1957	1977	1979	1981	1983	1985
Median age (years)	37.0	32.4	32.8	33.6	34.4	35.8
Median income ($)	7,300	22,700	28,110	39,196	35,987	42,396
Median home price ($)	17,100	44,000	58,000	72,000	65,000	75,000
Median downpayment (percent of home price)	32.7	20.4	21.2	22.4	18.5	18.8
Median percent of income spent on mortgage payment	15.0	14.4	17.1	19.1	17.5	16.2
Average term to maturity of loan (years)	19.0	26.2	27.4	26.4	26.0	26.0
Annual average rate of home price inflation during preceding 7 years (%)	8.1	10.1	11.8	10.4	8.5	6.2

Note: Mortgage payment does not include real estate taxes, utilities, or homeowners' insurance.

Sources: United States League of Savings Institutions; Federal Home Loan Bank Board; U.S. Department of Commerce; National Association of Realtors.

How are you going to pay for that house?

Today, a typical basic house with 1400 to 1600 square feet, three bedrooms, two baths, livingroom–dining area, two-car garage, located in a decent area, and close to schools and shopping costs about $87,000, as you'll see in Table 4.14. You'll pay for that house in two stages: (1) upfront and (2) long term. There are three steps upfront. When you first sign an agreement with the seller, you'll have to hand over some "earnest" money to show you're really serious about your commitment. How much depends on the seller and the price of the house. This is totally negotiable. Deals have been sealed with as little as $1,000.

Then you'll have to make the down payment. Depending on your credit rating, the down payment is typically around 20% of the price of the house. Obviously, the more money you can put down, the less you'll need to borrow and the smaller your monthly payments will be.

TABLE 4.14 Shelter: to buy or to rent?

City	Price Early 1987 ($)	Price Early 1986 ($)	Mortgage Interest Rate (%)	Typical Down Payment ($)	Closing Costs ($)	Annual Income Required ($)	Monthly Mortgage Payment ($)	Equivalent Monthly Rent ($)	Annual Interest Expense ($)	Tax Savings 28% bracket ($)	Tax Savings 38.5% bracket ($)
Atlanta	87,900	79,300									
Fixed rate mortgage			9.75	8,800	5,180	34,800	799	550–575	7,692	2,154	2,961
1-year ARM*			7.88	8,800	5,970	30,000	696		6,205	1,737	2,389
Boston	161,000	134,200									
Fixed rate mortgage			10.25	16,100	6,700	67,700	1,580	1,200–	14,817	3,704	5,705
1-year ARM*			8.38	16,100	7,200	59,700	1,393	1,300	12,193	3,386	4,694
Chicago	88,300	79,250									
Fixed rate mortgage			9.75	17,700	3,100	32,500	757	900–	6,865	1,922	2,643
1-year ARM*			7.75	4,500	3,100	28,200	656	1,050	5,450	1,526	2,098
Dallas	79,000	78,200									
Fixed rate mortgage			9.75	3,950	5,450	37,500	779	600–700	7,299	2,043	2,810
1-year ARM*			8.13	7,900	5,300	28,500	664		5,756	1,612	2,216
Los Angeles	150,000	138,575									
Fixed rate mortgage			9.75	30,000	2,900	49,100	1,226	1,000–	11,669	3,267	4,493
1-year ARM*			8.13	15,000	6,000	52,900	1,235	1,200	10,928	3,060	4,207
New York City	193,000	161,350									
Fixed rate mortgage			10.50	19,300	10,800	83,500	1,948	1,200–	18,197	5,095	7,006
1-year ARM*			8.88	19,300	11,300	75,100	1,753	1,300	15,367	4,302	5,916

TABLE 4.14 *(Cont.)*

City	Price Early 1987 ($)	Price Early 1986 ($)	Mortgage Interest Rate (%)	Typical Down Payment ($)	Closing Costs ($)	Annual Income Required ($)	Monthly Mortgage Payment ($)	Equivalent Monthly Rent ($)	Annual Interest Expense ($)	Tax Savings 28% bracket ($)	Tax Savings 38.5% bracket ($)
Philadelphia	71,890	69,800									
Fixed rate mortgage			9.75	7,190	4,110	30,000	700	650–700	6,292	1,762	2,422
1-year ARM*			8.13	7,190	4,460	26,820	626		5,238	1,467	2,017
Phoenix	80,500	78,700									
Fixed rate mortgage			9.75	8,050	4,100	29,700	693	650–675	7,045	1,973	2,712
1-year ARM*			7.88	8,050	4,100	25,500	595		5,683	1,591	2,188
Seattle	86,950	82,300									
Fixed rate mortgage			9.75	4,350	6,402	29,200	803	600–700	8,032	2,249	3,092
1-year ARM*			8.00	4,350	6,402	25,500	699		6,583	1,843	2,534
Average City, U.S.A.	87,290	80,825									
Fixed rate mortgage			9.75	8,740	4,800	33,450	780	750–900	7,638	2,139	2,941
1-year ARM*			8.00	8,740	5,000	25,150	587		6,250	1,750	2,406

*ARM = adjustable rate mortgage

Notes: Typical prices to buy or rent 1,400 to 1,600 square feet with three bedrooms, two-bath, single-family existing home in an above-average neighborhood. Closing costs are estimates. Monthly mortgage payment includes principal, interest, taxes, and insurance. All mortgages have 30-year terms. Adjustable rate mortgage interest figures are for first year.

Sources: Century 21 Real Estate Corp. and Century 21 Mortgage Corp.

Table 4.14, based on typical downpayments at the time those cities were surveyed, will give you some idea how much may be involved. If all goes well, you'll then incur expenses for legal, appraisal, and other services. So at the deal's close, you may easily add another few thousand dollars to your upfront costs.

Because most of us don't have tons of ready cash at hand—at least not enough to pay for a house—we'll also need to take out a long-term loan called a mortgage. The conventional mortgage carries a fixed interest rate that remains the same throughout the life of the loan, which is usually 30 years. With a 10% fixed interest rate mortgage, you'll have to pay around $600 a month to cover principal and interest for an $80,000 house.

Until recently, getting a conventional mortgage was a simple matter: you only needed to go to your local bank or savings and loan and take out a fixed-rate mortgage. But rising house prices and then high interest rates in the early 1980s made it all but impossible for most people to afford a house. From Table 4.12 you'll see that for about four years, families with median incomes were locked out of the market completely since they didn't have the income to qualify for a mortgage loan.

So lenders started developing alternatives that would lure back some buyers. Among the alternatives: the variable or adjustable-rate mortgage (ARM). As the name implies, these mortgages have changing interest rates that are adjusted once or twice a year, according to prevailing market rates. There is usually a ceiling on how high the rate can go, generally no more than 2% a year and 4% or 5% over the life of the loan. So a 10% rate will have a ceiling of 14% or 15%.

Then there's the rollover, where you can renegotiate the loan rate every three to five years, depending on the terms of your agreement. A third device, the graduated payment mortgage, starts you off with a smaller monthly payment than that required by a conventional loan, but it will increase over time. One disadvantage: you'll end up paying more money over the life of the loan.

No matter which type of mortgage you take out, a major percentage of the monthly payment during the early years of the loan will go toward the interest. With rates in the teens, you may find yourself paying a total that is in excess of three or four times the principal amount of the loan.

Don't give up or panic if you can't afford to buy a house on your own. There are other avenues you can explore. In fact, the common practice today is to put together a finance package from various sources. For example, if you don't have enough for a downpayment, you may borrow it from your parents, relatives, friends, or even some other third party. This may come as a straight loan, or as a joint venture, a partnership, where your partners will share with you the tax benefits and appreciation, if and when you sell the house. This same technique can be applied to the mortgage portion as well. Your realtor may have just such a program for you.

Another source of financial assistance is the seller. Let's say you fell in love with a $100,000 house. After a $20,000 downpayment, the bank will qualify you for only $60,000 at 13%. The seller, meanwhile, may be willing to help you by lending you the remaining $20,000 at 10%. But you'll have to pay this back in five to ten years. For example, you'll pay interest through those five years, then a "balloon" payment, meaning all of the principal at the end of the fifth year. The pitfall here is obvious: when the time comes, you'd better have the rest of the money or, at least, the ability to refinance the loan.

When mortgage interest rates finally dropped back to single digits in 1986, most of these alternative financing methods, except for ARMs, faded away as quickly as they appeared. Lower rates combined with higher income and soft house prices pushed the National Association of Realtors' housing affordability index to a record 110.8 in December 1986, the highest level since March 1978, when it was 111.9 (for more details, see Table 4.12). What this means is a family with the annual median income of $29,200 has more than enough—$2,836 to be exact—to qualify for a mortgage to pay for a median-priced ($80,600) existing home.

Table 4.15 shows at a glance how much house you can afford at varying family income levels, assuming a 20% down payment, as based on December's affordability conditions:

Should you buy a new or an old house?

The median price of a new house is $107,000, and $85,000 for an existing house. There are other differences more than the price. Normally, the new house will have unused appliances and systems and thus should be in fine working condition. It may also have insulation and energy-saving devices that were not available in older homes. But then, the new house tends to have only the bare minimum, from the amount of space you'll get to how things are finished off.

TABLE 4.15 How much house can you afford?

Annual Income ($)	Price of House ($)
20,000	61,300
30,000	91,900
40,000	122,500
50,000	153,100

Notes: According to Federal National Mortgage Association lending requirements, principal and interest payments for an 80% loan should represent no more than 25% to 28% of yearly gross family income. The National Association of Realtors follows this guideline in calculating its affordability index by assuming that 25% of family income is used for principal and interest payments.

The older homes, on the other hand, tend to be more spacious, may have more character, and often are built with better quality materials. Another big plus: the landscaping may be complete and mature, which saves you the time and expense of buying and cultivating trees and shrubs. The major drawback: you may have to do a great deal of renovation, such as replacement of faulty plumbing, or inadequate wiring or insulation.

"Two out of every five homes will have at least one serious defect when they go on sale," says Kenneth Austin, chairman of HouseMaster of America, the home inspection and warranty service firm. Even then, he adds that "due to reduced workmanship standards and lower quality building materials, many newer homes—despite modern styling and features—don't match up well against an older home that's received proper maintenance and care over the years."

Table 4.16 lists major home defects, how often they occur, as well as the types of equipment that may be affected and what it costs to have them repaired or replaced.

Generally, the older the house, the more fixing up it will require. If you're considering an old house, it will definitely be worth your while to have it carefully inspected by experts. Make sure they list everything that needs to be repaired or replaced, when, and at what cost. For a typical home, this inspection will cost about $200 to $250.

TABLE 4.16 How much major home defects may cost you

Item	Age of Home			Equipment/ Service	Price to Repair/ Replace ($)
	1–12 years (%)	13–29 years (%)	30 years and older (%)		
Mixed plumbing pipes	0.0	6.7	39.3	Replumb Shower pan	2,000–3,000 900–1,600
Leaking in the basement	25.4	27.1	38.8	Water-proofing Sump pit and pump	2,500–3,000 600–800
Inadequate roof insulation	7.3	26.3	37.1	Wall insulation Attic insulation	2,500–3,000 800–1,100
Heating deficiences	7.8	19.7	29.0	Water boiler Warm air furnace	1,800–2,500 1,500–2,000
Plumbing defects	8.2	16.2	24.3	Shower pan Hot water heater	900–1,600 300–400
Poor roofing	0.7	18.9	22.6	Wood shingle roof Asphalt shingle roof	3,500–4,500 1,400–2,000
Cooling deficiences	7.7	11.9	12.9	Replace air-conditioning system Compressors	1,800–2,000 750–1,000
Electrical defects	12.8	9.2	10.7	Electrical service upgrade Add 220 volts/lines	600–1,000 250–400
Foundation deficiences	4.9	4.6	8.0	Major repair/ rebuild Underpin	4,000–6,000 3,000–6,000

Source: HouseMaster of America, 421 W. Union Avenue, Bound Brook, NJ 08805, (201) 469-6565.

Who can help you find that dream house?

Whether you're looking for a new or an older home, chances are the person who can help you most will be a reliable licensed real estate agent. Ask around for recommendations. Find someone who is a member of the National Association of Realtors, knows the area you're considering, and has a good number of houses available in your price range.

A real estate agent performs a variety of services, which includes arranging appointments, showing homes, and helping you determine which ones will suit your needs best. They can also tell you about the community, the schools, the shopping areas, and how much tax you'll be paying. But a realtor's biggest contribution is to come up with sources of mortgage money and to qualify you for financing upfront so there won't be any nasty surprises later on, a step that can be a real time saver. For all these services, a realtor gets a fee—one that's negotiable—but often runs about 6% of the selling price. This is usually included in the asking price.

On occasion, you may not need the services of a realtor, for example, when you're purchasing a new home from a builder who has prearranged financing for prospective buyers.

Where do you look for that dream house? Many experts consider location to be the single most important factor to consider when buying a house. A good location is more than just an attractive area. It should also be convenient to places such as shopping areas, public transportation, or work that are important to you. In addition, consider the type of neighborhood, the schools, the property tax, and the zoning.

You can get more for your money in some areas than others: this varies from city to suburb, from urban to rural areas, and from state to state. For example, the median price of an existing home in the United States is $85,000. In California or New York City, you'll have a hard time finding anything for much less than $100,000, but in Ohio or Michigan, you may still come up with some good prospects at half that price.

So how much house do you want? That depends on your needs, and to some extent, on your likes and taste. Do you want a bungalow or one with two or three floors? How many bedrooms? Bathrooms? Fireplaces? Are you fussy about having a separate dining room? Much may depend on the type of furnishings you already own.

Before you go searching for that dream house, compile a list of all your requirements. It may be useful to have two columns: one for the must items, and the other for things you're willing to compromise.

What happens when you've found that dream house?

You'll sign a purchase agreement with the seller and hand over a binder fee. Most offers today include a contingency clause that says you'll get this fee back if you can't get financing. Make sure this clause is included *before* you sign.

To help you with all the negotiations, it's a good idea to have a lawyer to represent you. His fee may vary from $200 to a few thousand, depending where you are located and how much work is involved.

Once you've signed with the seller, you'll have to finalize your financing arrangements. There'll be a title search, which ensures that no one else owns the property. This involves a one-time fee, ranging from about $400 to $800. Then your lawyer will draw up a deed formally conveying the title of the property to you.

At the closing, you'll get a bill listing all the items you'll be responsible for paying. This includes the title insurance, the legal, and other fees of the lender, and so forth. Depending on your location, the total of all these fees, together with the down payment, can easily add up to anywhere from about 5% to over 12% of the price of the house. By the time you're through with all this, you may discover that being a proud house owner is the quickest way to become a pauper. But don't despair—at tax time your new home may well become your best tax shelter.

Using your home as a tax shelter

Tax reform left intact the numerous tax benefits that homeowners may reap. If you file the long 1040 form, you may claim the mortgage interest and the real estate taxes you pay as itemized deductions. Even as tax reform cuts the top tax rate to 38.5% from 50%, individuals with high income brackets can still realize substantial savings.

For example, if you are in the 38.5 bracket, the aftertax cost of $1,000 a month in interest payments is only $615. Table 4.14 shows how much you may save in the 28% and 38.5% tax brackets (look at the last two columns).

Note, however, for mortgages obtained after August 17, 1986, there will be a limit to the amount you can deduct—up to the purchase price plus any cost of improvement. An exception to this is made when, for example, the proceeds are used to pay for educational or medical expenses. Then you can deduct up to the fair market value of the property. Also tax deductible are the real estate taxes paid on these homes.

To cope with the limitations required by tax reform, it is now all the more important to keep careful records. You'll need them if you want to maximize mortgage interest deductions, and when you want to sell, so you can adjust the basis used to calculate the gain. Knowing the types of improvements that qualify will help you to make the most of this provision. Generally, these are limited to capital improvements such as trees, shrubs, storm windows and doors, structural changes, an asphalt driveway, and many other inside and outside improvements or additions.

If you or a dependent have a medical problem requiring special equipment, you may be able to claim a medical deduction for certain improvements made to your home, which includes the cost of maintaining and operating them. In recent years, the courts have held, for example, that elevators for heart patients or swimming pools for polio victims are deductible to the extent that the cost of their installation exceeds the increase in the home's fair-market value.

Then when it's time to sell your house, you may exclude up to $125,000 of the gain, provided you're age 55 or over.

Using your home as a bank

Under tax reform your home may well be your most convenient source of cash, especially if you've already accumulated substantial equity in it. Here's how this works: get a home equity loan or line of credit and, just like a first mortgage, this interest is also deductible, up to the purchase price of the house plus improvements. However, if you use the proceeds to pay for education or medical expenses, you may deduct up to the fair market value of the property.

Proceeds may also be used for investments, but the deduction will be subject to the limits that apply to investment expenses. Under tax reform, miscellaneous expenses, which include those spent on invest-ments, now have to meet a 2% floor on AGI before they are deductible. So if your AGI is $25,000, your miscellaneous expenses will have to be in excess of $500 before you can start deducting.

If you think a home equity loan is too good to be true, the banks and thrifts obviously think so too. Since the 1986 Tax Reform Act was passed, they've been heavily promoting these loans and coming out with new products tied to it. A recent addition: a home equity loan tied to a credit card. Before you sign up for such a line of credit, read the fine print carefully.

For more details about the high costs of home equity lines, please turn to Chapter 5.

To enjoy or to rent your vacation home?

Although tax reform left intact the mortgage interest deduction for second homes, you should be aware that a distinction is now being made between using or renting it. As the tax benefits may vary greatly between the two methods, you should spend a little time on this question and figure out which one will give you maximum savings. Which strategy is better depends largely on the amount of mortgage interest that's being paid, compared with the rental income received.

Generally, many people with high incomes—say, in the six fig-ures—may fare better by using their vacation homes rather than renting them after 1987. This is because tax reform makes it tougher to claim the mortgage interest deduction on a vacation home. To qualify as a second residence, you must use it yourself—renting doesn't count any more—and you must use it for more than 14 days a year or 10% of the time it is rented. Otherwise, the mortgage interest will be consid-ered personal interest and subject to new deductibility limits. These will be phased out over five years so that by 1991 all personal interest will be nondeductible. Meanwhile, you will be able to write off 65% for 1987, 40% for 1988, 20% for 1989, and 10% for 1990.

On the other hand, renting will now give you only write-offs in expenses, and even those are limited to the amount of the rental income. This contrasts sharply with pre-tax-reform days when you tended to fare better renting than using your vacation home. The reason: in addition to deducting mortgage interest and real estate taxes, you were allowed to write off more expenses than the amount of rental income received, as long as you limited your personal use of the house to 14 days or 10% of the number of days it was rented out during the year.

Tax reform has now disallowed many of these write-offs, including a new rule that says losses from tax shelters will be considered "passive" and can only be used to offset passive income from shelters not to reduce income from wages and dividends. An exception, however, is made for rental real estate, which includes vacation homes.

If your AGI is under $100,000 and you actively manage your property, you can offset up to $25,000 a year in rental real estate losses against your other income.

TRANSPORTATION

While most car prices in the last five years have gone up 40% or more, median family income has increased only 21%. The current average price of a new car is about $15,000. No wonder that for most people, the family car is the fourth largest budget item after housing, taxes, and food. As a result, people who don't own cars already are thinking twice before they dash out and buy one. And for those who are already owners, more of them are choosing to keep their old cars or to trade them in for late-model used ones.

Assuming you do need a car, there are alternatives to buying one. For example, if you're only a week-end driver, it may make more sense to rent one. On the other hand, if you use your car for business, you may find it more advantageous to lease than to buy.

How much does it cost to own a car?

When you buy a car, paying for it is just the start. As a car owner, you'll also have to consider how much it costs to operate and maintain it. These expenses can be divided into two types: fixed and variable.

The fixed costs are those you must pay regardless of whether you drive the car or not. These include: depreciation, that is, the difference between the actual purchase price of the car and its resale value; insurance, a subject we'll explore in greater detail in the next section; interest paid on a car loan; as well as inspection charges, licensing, and registration fees.

The variable costs are the actual operating expenses of your car. These include what you'll need to keep the car going such as gasoline, oil, spark plugs and tires, and what you'll need to spend on maintenance and repair to keep it in good condition.

According to the American Automobile Association, a 1987 American-made car driven 15,000 miles a year for four years will cost an average of 24.6 cents a mile to operate. Table 4.17 gives more details on the trend for automobile ownership and operating costs.

TABLE 4.17 Car operating costs

Year	Cost per Mile (¢)	Type of Car
1950	6.8	Based on Ford, Chevrolet, Plymouth
1960	9.3	Chevrolet 8-cylinder Bel Air
1965	9.1	Chevrolet 8-cylinder Bel Air
1975	14.3	Chevrolet 8-cyclinder Malibu Classic
1980	21.2*	Chevrolet 8-cyclinder Malibu Classic
1981	24.0*	Chevrolet 8-cyclinder Malibu Classic
1982	24.4*	Chevrolet 6-cyclinder Citation
1983	23.8*	Chevette 4-cyclinder/Malibu/Impala 6-cyclinder
1984	23.0*	Chevette 4-cyclinder/Celebrity/Impala 6-cyclinder
1985	23.2*	Chevette 4-cyclinder/Celebrity/Impala 6-cyclinder
1986	23.2*	Chevette 4-cylinder/Celebrity/Caprice 6-cylinder
1987	24.6*	Chevette 4-cylinder/Celebrity/Caprice 6-cylinder

*Cost includes finance charges.

Source: American Automobile Association, Falls Church, VA.

What kind of car to buy

What car to buy depends on what you want and how much you're willing to spend. The average new car now sells for about $15,000. A used car is about half that. Whether you buy a new or a used car, keep in mind that the ideal car will have good crash test results, high gas mileage, low preventive maintenance and repair costs, as well as low insurance premiums and a high resale value. Unfortunately, no one car possesses all these attributes, so you'll have to weigh which of these qualities are most important to you and then find a car that fits those needs.

Whether to buy a big or a small car depends on the type of travelling you do. For long-distance driving, a big car is more comfortable but less fuel efficient. For running errands around town, a subcompact makes good sense and it's also easier to park. Whether new or used, big or small, just remember: the longer you own your car, the less per mile it will cost you to operate it. However, large cars cost more than small ones and new cars cost more than used ones.

Where to shop for that car

Before you go shopping for that car, it's a good idea to do some homework first. *The Car Book 1988*, by Jack Gillis (Harper & Row, $9.95), available at public libraries and bookstores, is a good reference to check out. Make a list of what you really want. This is one way to avoid being sold extra options, which can easily add 30% to 50% to the car's price.

Where to shop depends on how much work you're willing to do yourself. The lazy man's way is to use one of the car-buying services. For a fee of about $200, an outfit such as Automotive Search Inc. in suburban Bethesda, MD, will shop and haggle on your behalf. Some branches of the American Automobile Association also offer a similar service to its members. For an annual fee of $24, you can be a member of AAA, which also entitles you to a host of other services including towing, maps, and a vast collection of printed material on car-related topics.

The more traditional way is to seek out a reputable local dealer, one that will offer you good service even after the purchase. If you do your own bargaining, keep in mind the dealer's profit on large cars is about 15% of the window price; on smaller cars, it's around 8% to 14%. Try to do your auto purchasing, financing, and insuring separately. It's generally cheaper this way than to have the dealer do it all for you.

Auto insurance is a major cost of car ownership. This can vary greatly depending, for instance, on your age, sex, where you live, how long you've had a license, your previous record, and what you use your car for. Even the kind of car you own will affect your insurance bill since insurers often offer discounts on cars that pass crash tests with flying colors. So in shopping for cars, check out first those that qualify for a cheaper insurance rate.

For more ideas on ways to save, read the next section on insurance.

How are you going to pay for that car?

To attract buyers, the American auto manufacturers have increasingly been offering very attractive loan terms or rebates, or both. So check out what the dealership is offering before you dash to your local bank for a loan. Compare costs by working out the numbers to see which saves you more in the long run: a low rate or the rebate.

INSURANCE

It's human nature to want maximum financial protection for yourself and your family. But like all things financial, you should not let emotions alone dictate your decision. Buying the appropriate amount of insurance at the right price, requires some careful planning and searching around.

What is insurance?

Insurance is simply buying financial protection or coverage against future disasters such as death, sickness, or theft by paying a predetermined fee, called a *premium*. Always remember: a company that sells insurance is a business like any other—they're there to make money. By looking at the demographics, they can estimate the number of people in the different age groups who will die or have car accidents this year. From these probabilities, they'll be able to calculate the total they'll have to pay out, as well as the expenses they'll incur and the amount of profit necessary to make it all worthwhile. In short, the premiums you'll pay are carefully worked out to ensure they're playing the odds to their favor. Insurance companies take risks seriously: they will issue only policies that present minimum risk to them. That's one reason why some people with specific problems that are considered high risk, can never get insurance, even if they're willing to pay any price.

Like any business, insurance companies are always coming out with new products. Let's take a look at the major types and how you can figure out what insurance you need and how much.

Life insurance

Basically, there are two types of life insurance: term and whole life. But in recent years, there's a third type competing for your business—universal life—which started off as an alternative to whole life but is becoming more like term. Says Andrew Gold of A.M. Best, "universal life is designed to do everything: it can be term and it can be whole life."

Term, generally the least expensive of the three, covers you for a specific period of time. If you should die during this period, death benefits are paid to your beneficiaries. Common types of term policies include

- Straight term provides insurance for a certain number of years, say, five or ten; premiums may remain the same or may vary, in which case, it will start low and go up gradually. Most term policies are renewable. That is, after a certain period, say ten years, you have the right to renew your policy for another term. If you should become uninsurable, for example, if you discover heart trouble during this period, you can still get coverage for the next ten years.

- Decreasing term provides coverage that decreases with your premiums remaining constant. Let's say your premium is $500 a year, which may give you $150,000 of coverage in the early years and then gradually decrease with each succeeding year. If you require a great deal of coverage now since you have young children, but you'll need much less later on, then you may decide decreasing term is the route to go.

- Or you may opt for convertible term, which gives you the option to convert at some later date. What this means is you'll start off with a large term policy, at a time when you require a great deal of coverage. As your need decreases, you'll convert it to a smaller policy.

Because whole life attempts to give you both life and death benefits, it's more expensive than term. Part of your premium goes toward a cash surrender fund, which acts much like a forced savings plan. Remember, you're paying a price to have this savings feature. So if you're a disciplined person and can save on your own, you'll do much better by separating your investing from your insurance.

Like term, whole life comes in a variety of forms. The most common ones are

- Continuous premium or straight life, where your premium remains the same throughout the life of the policy. In this case, the younger you are, the lower the premium.
- Limited pay life is a form of straight life, but you pay premiums for only a set number of years or until you reach a certain age. Then you stop paying premiums, but your insurance remains in force until your death. Because your premium is paid up in a limited number of years, this is an expensive way to get insurance. So unless there's some good reason why you must be paid up at a particular time, don't buy limited pay life.
- Single premium means exactly what it says: you make a one-time payment to buy a certain amount of insurance to cover the rest of your life. This is used mostly for estate planning purposes. Let's say a surviving spouse just inherited a large estate. To ensure there'll be something to pass on to the children, he or she will get a single-premium policy large enough to pay all estate taxes, in case of death.

There are some other common types of life insurance that you should know something about.

- Credit or mortgage life insurance is basically term insurance, designed to cover loans that are outstanding. Generally speaking, this is a costly way to get insurance. Your best bet is to get a large enough regular term policy to cover all your needs, including debts, rather than get a separate one to cover just credit or mortgage loans.
- Group life insurance is commonly term insurance that is available through your employer or through a business or social membership organization. Being in a group gives you certain advantages: the rates are usually lower, no physical exam is required, and often all family members can be included. But there are also disadvantages. If you should change jobs, retire, or be laid off, you may suddenly find yourself without coverage. So don't just rely on group life—use it as a supplement to your basic coverage.

- Endowment life insurance covers you for a set number of years—say, 20 years—or until age 60 when you can redeem the policy for its face value. If you die, your beneficiary will get the guaranteed sum. Because the stress here is on savings, the premium for an endowment is higher than for straight life. Here again, it's more cost effective to keep your insurance separate from your investments.

Do you need life insurance?

Most people need some life insurance. But at different seasons of life, you'll need varying amounts. For example, as a single working professional your life insurance needs should be minimal—just get enough to cover your debts and funeral expenses. When you start having a family of your own, then it's time to get sufficient insurance to cover them, in case something happens to you. As most families now have two incomes, this burden is increasingly shared between two breadwinners instead of one.

The more difficult question to answer is: How much insurance do you need? There's really no set rule, although life insurance agents will try to sell you amounts based on varying approaches. Among them is the multiple-earnings approach. This takes your current gross annual earnings and automatically multiplies it by seven. So if you're earning $30,000 a year, you may need $210,000 of life insurance. There is also the life-value approach, which calculates how much money you'll earn in your working life and then discounts this figure to current dollars.

The main problem with both these methods is they do not really take your individual needs into account, which brings us to the third method. This requires you to do some thinking to figure out what your specific needs are in case you die. First, estimate your financial needs—these should include money to pay debts, income to support dependents until the last one is self sufficient, as well as special funds for emergencies, education, or estate taxes. Then take a look at your resources. Most of us will find that what we have will not be sufficient to cover these needs and we'll have to resort to insurance to fill in the gap. Why not use the worksheet in Table 4.18 to work out your own life insurance needs?

TABLE 4.18 How much life insurance do I need?

1. List your resources—if you completed a net worth statement in Chapter 2, the asset column will help you here.

Resource	Amount/Value ($)
Savings	
Investments	
Real Estate	
Life Insurance	
Others: pension	
social security	
Total resources	

2. List your needs—if you did a family budget in Chapter 3 that will be a great help here. Take the annual budget and multiply it by the number of years in which you expect to have dependents staying with you at home to determine your required income.

Annual budget × Number of years = Income required

$_____ × _____ yrs. = $_____

Need	Amount Outstanding/Required ($)
Debts	
Installment loans	
Charge accounts	
Home mortgage	
Funeral expenses	
Education for kids	
Emergencies	

TABLE 4.18 *(Cont.)*

Need	Amount Outstanding/Required ($)
Estate taxes	
Other	
Total needs	

3. By subtracting your total needs from your total resources, you will get an idea of the amount of life insurance you should buy.

Total needs	$	_____
Total resources	−	_____
Amount of life insurance		_____

In addition to life insurance, most of us should also consider having some health and disability insurance. Being sick or disabled in America can easily bankrupt you. So it's a good idea to have some coverage, which is normally available from where you work. If not, check out business or social associations where you may get group rates—usually these are lower than you'll have to pay individually.

Other types of insurance you may want to check out include household policies for theft, fire and casualty, and car insurance.

How to save on insurance

One of the most effective ways to reduce your insurance cost is to carry a higher deductible. This is the amount you're responsible for paying when there's a claim. So, if you have a $200 deductible and a loss of $400, you'll pay the first $200 and the insurer will pick up the rest. As you increase your deductible, the insurer will lower your premium. For example, if you were to increase your deductible for the comprehensive coverage of your car to $100 from $50, you'd save about 20% of your premium.

By paying your premiums annually rather than monthly, you can save 5% to 10% of your total cost. To avoid having to pay all your insurance bills at the same time, spread them out so you can meet your payments with your monthly income.

Where possible, get one big policy rather than lots of little ones. In addition to being hard to keep track of, you'll also be paying higher fees. Check and see if you can add a rider to an existing policy before you buy a new one. For example, you pay less for a rider to a decreasing term policy than getting a completely separate one.

Most important of all, no matter what type of insurance you're interested in, do shop around. Rates can vary greatly from company to company. Your aim should be to get what you need at the lowest cost possible.

TAKING THE NEXT STEP: WHERE TO GET HELP

Whether you simply need more information or help to solve a problem, the resources in Table 4.19 will come in handy.

TABLE 4.19

Source	What's Available
AUTOS	
American Automobile Association 8111 Gatehouse Road Falls Church, VA 22047 (703) 222-6332	A federation of more than 160 motor clubs that provides members with a full range of auto- and travel-related services, plus educational and legislative activities to further the interests of all car owners and other travelers.
AutoCAP 8400 Westpark Drive McLean, VA 22102 (703) 821-7144	Complaint mediation services to handle disputes between consumers and dealers. Sponsored by the National Automobile Dealers Association, AutoCAP runs 47 such centers around the country.
Changing Times Auto Guide Cars' 87 1729 H Street NW Washington, D.C. 20006 (202) 887-6400	An annual listing of all new cars, plus tips on smart buying and financing, insurance, leasing, and tax breaks. Available at bookstores, newstands or by mail ($3.50).
Insurance Institute for Highway Safety Communications Department Watergate 600 N.W. Washington, D.C. 20037 (202) 333-0770	Information about crashworthiness, collision claims, and theft histories of various cars, plus performance records of such products as air bags, seat belts, and children's car seats.

TABLE 4.19 *(Cont.)*

Source	What's Available
National Highway Traffic Safety Administration U.S. Department of Transportation 400 Seventh Street S.W. Washington, D.C. 20590 (800) 424-9393 (202) 366-0123	Information on safety topics such as auto recalls and defective tires.

REAL ESTATE

Source	What's Available
Home Owners Warranty (HOW) 2000 L Street N.W. Washington, D.C. 20036 (800) 841-8000	Free brochures on what to do to maintain your house or to remodel it, plus a list of HOW members, who are required to build according to approved standards and back this up by providing 10-year protection against major defects on the new houses they build.
HSH Associates Ten Mead Avenue Riverdale, NJ 07457 (201) 831-0550	A *Homebuyer's Kit* ($12) that will tell you everything you need to know on how to shop for a mortgage, including a list of lenders near you that are offering the most competitive rates. As lenders are surveyed weekly, you can get an updated list ($6) whenever you need it.
National Association of Home Builders Department of Consumer Affairs 15th and M Streets N.W. Washington, D.C. 20005 (202) 822-0200	Dispute resolution between member builders and buyers of both new and existing houses. Will act only on written requests that have the proper documentation. This means copies of checks, warranties, and anything else that will back up your transaction.
National Association of Realtors 777 14th Street N.W. Washington, D.C. 20005 (202) 383-1063	Trade group for realtors. There are local boards in most major cities. Check your yellow pages for the branch nearest you.

INSURANCE

Source	What's Available
American Council of Life Insurance Information Services 1001 Pennsylvania Ave. N.W. Washington, D.C. 20004 (202) 624-2000	General information or answers to questions about life and health insurance. For complaints, the council will direct you to the right government agency.

TABLE 4.19 *(Cont.)*

Source	What's Available
A.M. Best Oldwick, NJ 08858 (201) 439-2200	The Life/Health division publishes insurance guides, such as *Best's Flitcraft Compend, Best's Review* (a monthly), and the biannual *Retirement Income Guide* (an analysis of annuities).
Insurance Information Institute 110 William Street New York, NY 10038 (800) 221-4954	Information or answers to queries on property and casualty insurance. When the institute can't help you, it will try to refer you to someone who can.

TAXES

Source	What's Available
The Brennan Report P.O. Box 882 Valley Forge Office Colony Valley Forge, PA 19482 (215) 783-0647	A monthly newsletter on tax-advantaged investments and tax planning ($145/year).
Internal Revenue Service Taxpayer Ombudsman C.PRP, Room 3316 1111 Constitution Ave., N.W. Washington, D.C. 20224 (202) 566-6475	The ombudsman's job is to intercede on the taxpayer's behalf. The local IRS offices, where a variety of tax publications and forms are available, solve individual problems. At tax time, you may want to request IRS's Publication 17, *Your Federal Income Tax*. It's one of the best how-to manuals on the market and it's free.
U.S. Tax Court 400 Second Street N.W. Washington, D.C. 20217 (202) 376-2754	Information about how to represent yourself at the U.S. Tax Court by writing or phoning the clerk of the court for a package of materials that includes all the necessary forms, a list of cities where the court sits, plus a booklet explaining small tax case procedure in plain English.

5

Credit:
How Much Is
Too Much?

Fall is often the time of year when financial centers send letters to prospective customers offering preapproved lines of credit that typically range from $2,000 to $10,000. Usually, a credit or debit card is also part of this offer so you can do all your Christmas shopping now and pay later. It's flattering to be the recipient of so much credit, but watch out that it doesn't turn into a nightmare. As most people know, signing up is easy, but once you have credit, it's always a temptation to use it. And if you have too many such accounts, you may inadvertently overextend yourself.

HOW TO FIGURE YOUR DEBT THRESHOLD

Institutions that offer you credit are often only concerned with what's due to them, not what you owe in total. If, at this moment, you do not know the exact amount of what you owe, make a list immediately and monitor it carefully. Your list should include not just the obvious items such as mortgage or car loans, but also the less obvious such as the borrowings from an insurance policy or interest due to IRS.

Just as we all have a threshold on risk, we also have a threshold on debt. How much debt can you live with comfortably? You will get some idea by filling in Table 5.1 which covers the major items that affect most of us.

As a general rule of thumb, lenders now require that no more than 28% of your gross income be spent on housing expenses and 8% of gross income for all other loans. But in practice, it's a bit more involved than that as the following example will illustrate.

For someone who earns $25,000 a year, lenders say $7,000 can be spent for mortgages and $2,000 for all other loans. This leaves only about $16,000 for other expenses. However, for someone who earns $100,000 a year, spending $28,000 for housing and another $8,000 on miscellaneous loans would still leave $64,000 to cover other expenses. How much you earn will play a big part on whether the lenders' rule will fit your needs, or whether it's better for you to come up with your own set of percentages.

TABLE 5.1　How much credit?

Item	What Lenders Allow	What You're Comfortable With	Do You Really Need it?
House			
Home equity line			
Car(s)			
Bank credit cards			
Nonbank credit cards, (American Express, Discover)			
Other credit cards (gas, store)			
Other			
TOTAL LOANS:			

TO BORROW OR NOT TO BORROW?

While interest on your savings has been coming down to Eisenhower-era rates, the cost of money for certain types of loans has remained pretty constant. As Table 5.2 illustrates, while money market accounts are paying around 5.5%, the average revolving credit card is still charging in excess of 18%. Under such conditions, it's best to pay up every month, and do your borrowing elsewhere at more favorable rates.

TABLE 5.2 What you earn versus what you pay

What You Earn		What You Pay	
Type of investment	Yield (%)	Type of loan	Rate (%)
Money market accounts	5.69	Revolving credit cards	18.83
6-month CDs	7.02	Unsecured personal loans	14.53
1-year CDs	7.42	New auto loans	10.40
2½-year CDs	7.86	Home equity loans	10.46
5-year CDs	8.38	Adjustable-rate mortgage	8.01
10-year Treasury bond	9.56	15-year fixed mortgage	10.72
30-year Treasury bond	9.72	30-year fixed mortgage	11.13

Notes: As of end of September 1987. ARMs adjustable annually.
Sources: Bank Rate Monitor, HSH Associates and Salomon Bros.

THINK BEFORE YOU CHARGE

As we enter the post-tax-reform era, the common practice of spend first, pay later may need some rethinking. Take the subject of plastic.

Now that interest on revolving credit is no longer fully deductible—for 1987, you will be able to write off only 65%, with the percentage dropping to zero by 1991—it pays to get a grip on your credit cards. Once again, knowing something about the card business will help you to decide which one to pick.

In the U.S. today, there are a total of 731 million credit cards issued to 105.5 million holders, averaging 6.9 cards per person. Over 70% of these cards are proprietary, that is, they are issued by telephone or gasoline companies, retail stores, car rentals, and others for use at their own facilities. The remaining 29% are 210.1 million general-purpose cards, of which the bulk—some 186 million—are issued by Visa and MasterCard member banks to 75.5 million consumers, or an average of 2.46 cards per person. The rest is taken up by American Express, Sears, and Citicorp, which owns Diners Club, Carte Blanche, and Choice.

According to The Nilson Report (the news and advisory service for the credit/debit-card industry), half of all bank cards in the U.S. are issued out of just five states: California, New York, South Dakota, Delaware, and Illinois. One card in every four came from Citibank, Bank of America, Chase Manhattan, Manufacturers Hanover, First Chicago, or Chemical Bank.

Only about 5% of the nation's cards are issued by the four low-interest ceiling states—Arkansas, Connecticut, Texas, and Washington. Over half the bank-card holders in Arkansas and Texas, however, are using cards from one of the big out-of-state issuers charging higher rates. The reason: to keep losses manageable, banks in low-rate states have been rejecting half of all the applications they receive. In addition, many banks in these states have moved or have threatened to move their credit card operations to states with more liberal interest rates. As a result, many consumers have discovered it's risky to select a card from a low-rate state: chances of being rejected are great and, if accepted, you may one day suddenly learn the issuer has moved to another state.

Bank cards alone account for over half of the total U.S. credit card debt, which reached a new high of $84.4 billion in 1986. Of this, just over 16%, or $13.6 billion, is owed by convenience card users, who pay up monthly and thus incur no finance charges. The remaining $70.8 billion is owed by 36.9 million people who are the revolving credit users.

MAKING THE MOST OUT OF PLASTIC

Before you sign up for that piece of plastic, ask yourself two crucial questions. How much do you plan to spend each month? How are you going to pay for the purchases you charge? Basically, there are three types of card users: revolvers, who make minimal payments of as low as 2.5% of their outstanding monthly balance; average users, who alternate between paying in full one month and paying the minimum the next; and convenience users, who always pay in full.

To help you make the most of plastic, the Consumer Credit Card Rating Service of Santa Monica, CA, has compiled the *Credit Card Locator*, which acts much like a printed spreadsheet. Armed with the information about your own spending and paying habits, you can figure out from this chart exactly how much credit will cost you each year at varying interest rates and annual fees. Accompanying this spreadsheet is a survey of interest rates, fees and grace periods of over 500 cards issued by some 250 major institutions around the country.

Table 5.3 lists the top eight bank cards from the *Credit Card Locator–Spring 1987 Survey*, classified according to the three types of card users. To qualify for the best distinction, all issuers must meet four crucial criteria: (1) a demonstrated interest in building a nationwide card base, (2) a favorable interest-fee-grace-period combination, (3) a lack of geographic restrictions, and (4) a lack of deposit-relationship restrictions.

By knowing what type of card user you are, you can avoid annual fees and minimize finance charges by paying off balances within the grace period. For example, Table 5.3 shows that if you're a revolver, you should seek out low-interest issuers such as People's Bank in Bridgeport, CT. Assuming you charge $100 each month, the combined cost of annual fees and finance charges over a 12-month period at People's Bank will come to $79.52 a year versus $131.49 at First Interstate Bankcard in California, a 65% saving.

As an average user, your aim should be to find issuers with low or no annual fees, such as at U.S.A.A. Federal Savings Bank in San Antonio, TX. If you spend $250 a month, you'll incur an annual cost of $25.81 with U.S.A.A., less than half of the $56.51 at Chase Manhattan Bank.

Convenience users will also benefit most from a free card, such as those being offered at Imperial Savings of San Diego, CA, or First National Bank of Wilmington, DE.

As no one single card will suit all purposes, the smart shopper may opt to have two cards: one for revolving credit and the other for convenience use. For example, for cash advances, use the revolving credit card. The reason: you start paying interest immediately, so it's more economical to use a card that charges the lowest rate possible. For purchases you know you can pay in full at month's end, you'll use the free convenience card.

TABLE 5.3 The top eight bank cards

	Standard Cards				Premium Cards		
Issuer/ telephone/ city/state	Interest rate (%)	Annual fee ($)	Grace period (days)	Issuer/ telephone/ city/state	Interest rate (%)	Annual fee ($)	Grace period (days)
Revolving credit							
Higher balances							
People's Bank (800) 423-3273 Bridgeport, CT	11.5	20	25	Goldome FSB (800) 237-3703 Buffalo, NY	14.5	30	25
Lower balances							
Manufacturers Bank Wilmington (302) 366-8478 Wilmington, DE	13.6*	No fee	None	Fidelity Bank & Trust (800) 544-6666 Richmond, VA	15.9*	24	25
Average user							
U.S.A.A. Federal Savings Bank (800) 922-9092 San Antonio, TX	14.0*	No fee	25	Colonial National Bank (800) 223-3933 Wilmington, DE	17.9*	20	25

TABLE 5.3 The top eight bank cards

	Standard Cards				Premium Cards			
Issuer/ telephone/ city/state	Interest rate (%)	Annual fee ($)	Grace period (days)		Issuer/ telephone/ city/state	Interest rate (%)	Annual fee ($)	Grace period (days)
Convenience user								
Imperial Savings Association (800) 345-3263 San Diego, CA	19.8	No fee	25		First National Bank of Wilmington (800) 772-7779 Wilmington, DE	17.9*	No fee	25

*Variable rates.

Note: As of summer 1987.

Source: Consumer Credit Card Rating Service, Box 5219, Ocean Park Station, Santa Monica, CA 90405; (213) 392-7720; send $10.00 for a copy of the *Credit Card Locator.*

The Optima option

Now you also have the Optima option, a new service American Express started offering in the summer of 1987 to individual card members of good standing to extend payment on purchases at a very competitive initial variable interest rate of 13.5%.

But with this low rate comes a price: the Optima enhancement costs only $15 a year, but as you must also maintain one of the other cards, your total annual fees will be much higher than that—$60 for the green card members and $80 for the gold. Platinum holders, who pay $250 a year, get the Optima card free.

Unlike the other American Express cards where you generally have to pay in full, the Optima gives you the option to extend payment on purchases. You'll be assigned a line of credit individualized to meet your needs. If you opt to pay in full, you have 25 interest-free days. As usual for cash advances, you'll incur finance charges from the date of transaction.

On the surface, the 13.5% rate sounds very attractive. But since the rate is variable, you should look deeper to see what it may mean if rates were to trend upwards, as they seem to be doing already. Knowing how the rate is calculated will help: the rate will be set within a band of 1.7 to 1.8 times the prime rate as reported in the Wall Street Journal and adjusted seminannually. So if the prime goes up one point to 8.75%, your rate will jump to 15.75% (8.75% × 1.8). The prime was at 7.5% when American Express introduced the Optima with the 13.5% rate; within the month, the major banks raised the prime rate to 8.25%.

Most other variable rates simply add a certain number of points to the index involved. As Table 5.4 shows, this multiplier can produce some stunning effects when compared to other variables. For example, the House of Representatives' Subcommittee on Consumer Affairs proposed a cap on interest rates to be based on the return of 1-year Treasury securities, plus eight points. With 1-year Treasury yielding about 5.8%, add 8, and you get 13.8%. If the 1-year securities go up five points to 10.8%, the interest will rise to 18.8%. On the Optima card, however, a 5 point increase in the prime will send the interest rate up to 22.5%.

To help you decide whether the Optima is for you, Table 5.5, based on varying amounts spent every month, shows at a glance how total annual carrying costs—that is, annual fees plus finance charges—compare with other typical standard and premium revolving bank

TABLE 5.4 How the Optima multiplier may escalate

House Proposal			Optima		
When 1-year Treasury yields are at (%) . . .	+ 8	Rate is adjusted to (%) . . .	When prime is at (%) . . .	× 1.8	Rate is adjusted to (%) . . .
5.8	8	13.8	7.5	1.8	13.5
6.8	8	14.8	8.5	1.8	15.3
7.8	8	15.8	9.5	1.8	17.1
8.8	8	16.8	10.5	1.8	18.9
9.8	8	17.8	11.5	1.8	20.7
10.8	8	18.8	12.5	1.8	22.5

compare with other typical standard and premium revolving bank cards. The latter generally has minimum lines of credit that start at $5,000 and charges both a higher rate and fee. Except for Manufacturers Bank, Wilmington, which offers no grace period, all other cards listed give 25 interest-free days to users who pay their balances in full.

TABLE 5.5 Comparing Optima with other revolving bank cards

Institution	Current Rate (%)	Annual Fee ($)	Type of Card	Annual Cost of Card at Different Buying Levels($)		
				$100	$300	$600
American Express	13.5*	15 60	Optima with green	130.24	270.73	481.46
Typical standard cards People's Bank	11.5	20	Visa/ Mastercard	79.52	198.58	377.11
Manufacturers Bank, Wilmington	13.6*	0	MasterCard	69.77	209.32	418.64

TABLE 5.5 *(Cont.)*

Institution	Current Annual Rate (%)	Annual Fee ($)	Type of Card	Annual Cost of Card at Different Buying Levels ($)		
				$100	$300	$600
U.S.A.A. Federal Savings	14.0*	0	MasterCard	72.94	218.83	437.65
Sears Discover Card	19.8	0	Discover	104.78	314.34	628.67
Typical premium cards Goldome FSB	14.5*	30	Visa	105.65	256.94	483.89
Citibank Preferred	16.8	50	Visa	138.19	314.57	579.14

*Variable rates.

Note: As of March 31, 1987.

Sources: Consumer Credit Card Rating Service, Box 5219, Ocean Park Station, Santa Monica, CA 90405; (213) 392-7720; send $10 for a copy of the *Credit Card Locator.*

At $100 a month, the Optima ranks as the second most costly of the seven cards listed; at $600 a month, it ranks fourth. If you spend a lot, or if you travel abroad a great deal, you may find the Optima option worthwhile.

USING YOUR HOME AS A CHECKBOOK

Homeowners who previously ignored the bankers' plea to take advantage of the convenient, smart, inexpensive way to borrow money by taking out a home equity loan may now be more than tempted as banks continue to promote them by offering various incentives, which include rates as low as 7.5%.

"At these attractive rates, many consumers are rushing to sign up for these home equity lines of credit often on the assumption that one day they may need it," says Thomas E. Honey, president of the Consumer Bankers Association. Be warned, however, that convenience is not going to come cheap.

"They are not the ultimate solution to all your financial problems, as they've been made out to be," says loan expert Paul Havemann of HSH Associates.

Although a home equity loan can give you unprecedented access to credit, it is basically still just a second mortgage, secured by your home. However, unlike former times when such a loan reaped you a lump sum, all you get today is access to a line of credit. Most lenders will let you borrow no more than 75% to 85% of a house's appraised value, minus the balance remaining on the first mortgage. Once approved, the credit is there for you to use at your convenience. Depending on the type of account you have, you may access it with checks or even credit cards.

"However, unlike revolving credit or other unsecured debt where the lender is left holding the bag if the customer is overextended, the title to the home is at stake with these home equity loans," says Thomas Honey of the Consumer Bankers Association. In fact, a lien or a default on your first mortgage, and sometimes even a late payment, may trigger the institution that holds your home equity loan to exercise its right to demand immediate full payment of what you owe.

So don't expect the institutions to furnish discipline. If your current total debt payments are already close to 40% of gross income, then a home equity loan is not for you.

Most home equity lines carry variable rates, which means interest rises and falls with changing money market rates. The 1987 banking bill requires all variable-rate loans to have a cap. There is, however, no limit imposed on the cap. So if interest rates should trend upward again—as they did back in 1980, when the prime rate shot from 11% to 21.5% in just three months—your monthly payments may rise substantially and become unmanageable.

Although most home equity loans now charge no points, most do require a one-time application or origination fee that may range from $100 to $450. Upfront expenses will also include an appraisal fee of $200 to $350, plus closing costs that may average 1% to over 5%, which depends on where you live and the amount you borrow. For example, closing costs at Chemical Bank for $15,000 are $801 in New York City, but only $513 in Connecticut. For $200,000, the cost is $3,865 and $1,320 respectively.

There are also annual fees, which you'll have to pay whether you draw on your line of credit or not. Many institutions, mainly those from the west and midwest, are now charging an annual maintenance fee that may range from $20 to $50. They also recommend you take out insurance on the loan.

As more institutions offer a tier-rate structure, the larger the amount you borrow and use, the better the rate you'll be able to get. For example, at one point at Pathway Financial, NJ, if you borrowed and used from $5,000 to $25,000, you'd pay prime plus 1%; for $25,001 to $100,000, you'd pay just prime. At Bank of America, under $20,000, you might pay a rate equal to the 3-months CD plus 3.75%; from $20,000 to $49,999 you'd pay index plus 3.5%; from $50,000 to $500,000, index plus 3.25%.

Here are some other tips to keep in mind if you still decide to go shopping for a home equity loan:

- Start with your own local bank. As a customer your bank may have a special deal for you. For example, at Chase Manhattan, noncustomers recently paid prime plus 2.75%, while customers paid prime plus 1.75%.

- Think before you sign. First, identify your needs. Don't use home equity loans to finance current consumption. They make good sense if used for home improvements, education, or medical bills. Figure out the exact amounts you'll require, plus how and when you'll repay the loan. Keep in mind that the amount you plan to use should be large enough to justify the expenses and fees that are involved.

- Smaller monthly payments associated with equity loans can be deceptive. As these loans are typically amortized over 15 to 20 years, their monthly payments are relatively small. So even though the current rate may be low, over time, you may end up paying a great deal more. In addition, equity lines of credit can easily exceed $50,000, making available unprecedented buying power, which can easily be abused. Generally, total debt payments should not exceed 36% of gross income.

- Avoid "interest only" payments. To make the loans look extra attractive, most lenders will allow interest only monthly payments, deferring the principal to a later date. "While there may be occasions when a larger payment can't be afforded," Honey says, "you are probably overextended if you can't afford to pay down principal."

- Never borrow more than you can expect to repay over a reasonable period of time. Some lenders allow outstanding debt to be converted to a fixed amortization schedule, providing the discipline of monthly payments that you may prefer. Also make sure there are no prepayment penalties.

- Where alternatives exist, check them out first. Use the home equity line only as a last resort.
- Consult with your tax adviser to see if the interest payments on such a loan are really tax deductible for you.

For details about the tax deductibility of home equity loans, please see Chapter 4.

ALTERNATIVE WAYS TO BORROW

If you must borrow, check out some of the less obvious ways. For example

- If you have a brokerage account, you may be able to borrow amounts equal to 50% of the stocks and up to 80% of the bonds in your account. Interest on these margin loans fluctuate with market rates. Recently, it was about 10%.
- If you have universal or whole-life insurance coverage, you may be able to borrow the full amount of the cash value at rates as low as 5% or as high as 12%, depending on the type of policy and how old it is.
- A good temporary source of cash is your individual retirement account (IRA). Once a year, you're allowed to withdraw money from your IRA, but you must put it back within 60 days. Otherwise, you'll be liable for the income tax on the funds withdrawn plus a 10% penalty.

TAKING THE NEXT STEP: WHERE TO GET HELP

On questions or problems with credits or debits, the sources in Table 5.6 will be able to assist you.

TABLE 5.6

Source	What's Available
Associated Credit Bureaus P.O. Box 218300 Houston, TX 77218 (713) 492-8155	Credit bureaus, complaint resolution.
Consumer Credit Card Rating Service Box 5219, Ocean Park Station Santa Monica, CA 90405 (213) 392-7720	The *Credit Card Locator* ($10), which lists more than 500 bank cards at some 250 institutions nationwide.
Federal Trade Commission Bureau of Consumer Protection Pennsylvania Avenue at Sixth Street N.W. Washington, D.C. 20580 (202) 326-3240	Receives notice of complaints and violations against the Truth in Lending Act. For example, banks that fail to make full disclosure of their interest rates for loans; or mail-order houses and stores with deceptive advertising or unfair sales practices.
National Foundation for Consumer Credit 8701 Georgia Avenue, Suite 507 Silver Spring, MD 20910 (301) 589-5600	Credit counselling from a nonprofit agency with 280 offices around the country. Fees based on ability to pay; range is $0 to $50 but the average client pays only $10 to $12. Call or write with stamped, self-addressed envelope for information and the address of an office nearest you.

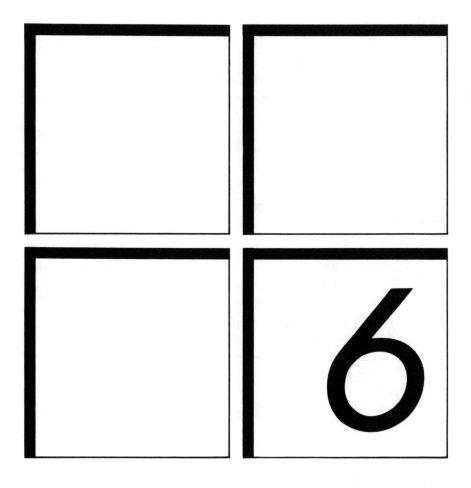

What
Is Investing?

Investing is accumulating assets and watching them grow. Investing requires taking a certain amount of risk. Generally speaking, the more risk you take, the greater your return. But unlike gambling or speculating, the risk you face in investing should be a calculated or educated one. Whatever you choose to put your money into, it's imperative you do some homework on it first to make sure it fits your temperament, that is, your own risk threshold and needs.

Most successful individual investors follow a specific strategy that they've devised for themselves and thus are comfortable with it. Basically, there are three types of investors:

1. Those who buy and hold; they put their complete faith in what they've selected and once they're into an investment they tend to hold it until it meets their goal, or some new development such as falling earnings prompts its disposal.

2. Those who go in and out of the market. These are the short-term traders who buy and sell continuously. To do this successfully, you must keep up to date with everything that's happening in the financial markets so you can move quickly and be a step ahead of the crowd.

3. Those who attempt to time their trades based on market trends—the timers or technicians who use charts to pinpoint the crucial buy-and-sell signals.

HOW TO START INVESTING

Because most investments cost a certain amount of money, before you can start investing you have to save. The only way to achieve financial independence is to do it with discipline and patience. It's a sound idea to include savings as an expense item in your budget.

Before you enter the world of saving and investing, you should know something about the concept of compound interest. Understanding compounding will help you to calculate the return on savings and investments, as well as on the cost of borrowing and the ravage of inflation on your gains.

SO WHAT IS COMPOUNDING?

It is, simply put, earning interest on interest. If you keep $10,000 in a savings account that pays 6% a year in interest, using annual compounding, at the end of the first year, you'll have $10,600, and at the end of the second year, you'll have $11,236 (106% × $10,600). By the end of five years, you'll have $13,382, ten years $17,908, 20 years $32,070 and so on.

Obviously, the more frequently compounding is used, the higher your annual yields will be. Table 6.1 shows what $10,000 at 8% a year will look like after five years of compounding, at different intervals.

TABLE 6.1 How the frequency of compounding makes a difference

Frequency of Compounding	Total ($)
Annually	14,693
Quarterly	14,859
Monthly	14,898
Weekly	14,914
Daily	14,919

Some banks can offer a higher nominal interest rate because they compound less frequently—and you end up with a lower effective annual yield. In checking out a savings product, always pay more attention to the yield. That is the true amount that your money will be earning.

To determine how long it takes to double a specific amount of money at a given rate with annual compounding, divide 72 by the interest. So a $10,000 account yielding 6% a year would double in 12 years (72 divided by 6).

WHAT'S THE FIRST STEP?

Save for an emergency fund first. How much to save depends on several factors. If both spouses work, probably three months' expenses will be sufficient; if only one works, then six months'. As the title implies, this fund is for emergency purposes. Keep this money liquid—in a money market fund, for example—so you can get your hands on it easily and without having to pay penalties in case of early withdrawal.

Once you've put aside an emergency fund, it's time to save and invest for specific purposes. Having set priorities makes saving and thus investing easier. Identify your goals clearly, calculate the amount you'll need, and set a timetable. Be realistic. It's always a good idea to have some goals that are short-term—for example, a trip to Europe or a Caribbean cruise in the winter—and some goals that are long-term— saving for the children's college education or your own retirement, for instance. This way, you don't have to wait so long for your dreams to come true that you actually get discouraged. It's always encouraging to see results. In short, try to balance your needs so you're working on both short- and long-term goals at the same time.

When you've figured out your priorities, it's time to take a look at what's out there that may fit your needs. Because this research is crucial, how well you do this may mean profit or loss later on. Here are some tips on how and what you should look at. After you've done it a couple of times, you'll be able to set up your own system.

Whether you're just starting out or looking for reinvestment ideas, no matter which investment vehicle you choose, your research involves basically the same three major areas.

1. What's the current economic climate?

    Because the financial markets are operated by people, they can behave erratically and react to news and rumors, sometimes without any really good solid reason for it. Knowing some of the signals that truly affect the markets will help you to decide which investments are timely and which are not. Let's explore the key ones here.

    ● Politics is one factor that requires some consideration. Studies have been done, for example, correlating presidential elections with how the market behaves. In 1973, David MacNeill, senior investment officer of a major Boston bank, devised a strategy that involved investing in stocks for the two years before an election and then switching to treasury bills for the next two years. This biannual switching strategy has produced excellent results for him: for the period November 30, 1962, to November 30, 1982, he achieved a 20-year return of 1423.2% versus a buy-hold return of 380%.

- Interest rates play a big role in our financial health. When rates are high, interest-sensitive industries, such as utilities and insurance companies, flounder. For the consumer, there's both good and bad news, depending on which side you're on. If it's income you're after, then high rates are good for you. On the other hand, if you're looking for money to borrow to buy a house then high interest rates may stymie your efforts.

- The dollar and how it compares with other currencies may also have an effect on how you may invest your money. Up through the second half of 1985, the dollar stayed unusually strong—continuing a trend that had lasted for a couple of years. At that time, the U.S. and its trading partners decided to gang up and drive the dollar down. The dollar then dropped 40% or more against the major currencies.

  For Americans who like to travel abroad, a strong dollar is a blessing, but for the U.S. economy it's really more of an albatross. The reason: foreign companies have a hard time trading with the U.S. and thus more goods are imported than are exported. This, in turn, adds to the U.S. trade deficit. For individuals who invest overseas, the possibility is always present that the eventual currency conversion back to the U.S. dollar may cancel out all the gains.

- Are company profits on the rise or decline? This gives you some hint of how companies are faring and their chances for good financial health.

- The inflation rate: will it stay low or drift higher once again? When you look at the return on an investment, it's always a good idea to consider the inflation rate as well. For example, if a 3-month Treasury bill yields 5% and inflation is at 2%, then your true return from this investment is really 3%. Also, if heavy transaction fees are involved, that should also be taken into consideration.

2. How to check out an investment

Ideally, start with an overview and then work down to the specific security. Once you've pinpointed the investment, it's also a good idea to compare it with other companies in the same industry. The following three steps will help you to assess an investment.

- The investment universe. This involves taking a look at the big picture—what's out there and how these investments have done in the past. Although past performance is no guarantee of future success, it does give you some idea of what to expect so you can make some educated estimate of its future.

- The chosen sector. From the universe, you'll select the sectors that fit your current needs. Let's say you decide on investing for income. You'll then examine closely all the investment vehicles—both short- and long-term—that will meet your objectives.

- The selected issues. From the chosen sector, you'll zero in on the specific individual issues that will become a part of your portfolio. Let's continue with the income example used before. You decide that for the short-term, you'll put your cash in a money market fund. Then, for the intermediate, you'll put some in a 2-year CD, and for the long-term, you'll buy some 10-year Treasury notes. In short, you'll apportion your assets among the selected issues and build a diversified portfolio of investments.

3. With whom are you dealing?

Your research should also include checking out with whom you'll be dealing, especially if it's a broker or salesman who comes soliciting your business. Before you part with your money, ask some questions. Insist on specific answers and not just evasive responses. Get to know the following:

- The firm. Who are the principals and officers? How about checking some references? Not just other investors but reputable and reliable recommendations, such as a bank or well-known brokerage firm that you can easily contact. Is the firm under any governmental or industry regulatory supervision? If disputes should arise, how can they be resolved?

- The investment. Can you get copies of any literature, prospectuses, or risk disclosure documents on the proposed investment? Is it traded on a regulated exchange? What risks are involved? Can it be easily liquidated if you decide that you need your money?
- The fees. Exactly how much of your money would go for commissions, management fees, and the like? Will there be other costs, such as interest or storage charges?

TAKING THE NEXT STEP: WHERE TO GET HELP

Please turn to Chapters 1 and 7 for sources and references on investing.

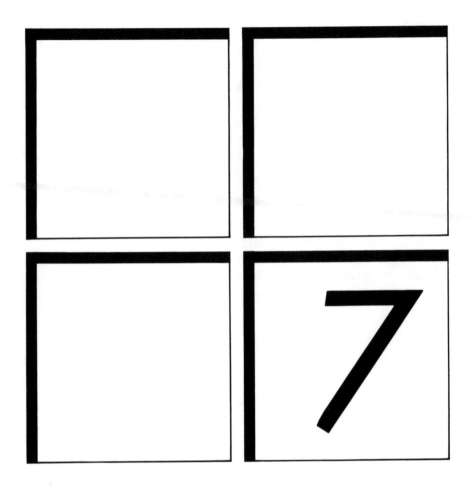

The Smorgasbord
of Investments

For most of us, the question of where to put our money is not so much a lack of investment vehicles out there to choose from, but more the problem of knowing which ones will suit our needs and objectives best. What makes it more complicated for individual investors is the influx of new products, often publicized by the sponsors. When checked closer, many products are really not so new, but rather a marketing gimmick to sell more of the same under a new name.

A good starting point is to know what the basic investment vehicles are, how they work, what's good or bad about them, what you can expect, and how they may or may not fit into your scheme of things. But because investment products are designed to meet certain objectives, it's crucial you know what your own criteria are so you can find ones that will match your needs.

Let's take a look at the three major objectives and the smorgasboard of investments under each category.

INVESTING FOR INCOME:
WHERE TO PUT YOUR SAVINGS

In these days of intense competition among financial centers for your money, where to put your savings is now no longer simply opening a passbook account at your local bank or savings and loan. In fact, the passbook account along with its 5.50% interest rate has been regulated out of existence with the final deadline for banking deregulation on April 1, 1986. Institutions may now set whatever rates they feel their markets will accept.

In addition to many differing rates on the market, you also have many more investment vehicles to choose from. These range from NOWs to SuperNOWs, money market investment accounts to money market funds, CDs and bonds of all types, both taxable and nontaxable. And all these are available from just banks and thrifts.

There are also other financial centers—brokerage firms, mutual funds and the federal government—that offer a similar array of savings vehicles, plus a host of other investments, including stock trading, which traditionally is not allowed at banking institutions. But this 1933 Federal law that barred banks from the securities business was formally challenged in March, 1987, by Chase Manhattan Bank when it introduced the Market Index Investment, a deposit account whose return is based on a percentage of the gain in the Standard & Poor's 500.

For example, a 1-year Market Index Investment, with no guaranteed interest rate, could earn up to 75% of the percent change in the S&P 500 index. The earnings could be less, if you sign up for a shorter term of three, six, or nine months, or opt for the guaranteed minimum 4% return a year.

To illustrate: in a recent 12-month period, the S&P 500 rose 27.97%. If the account had existed during this period, a 1-year deposit with the 4% guaranteed return would have earned 11.2% (the 27.97% increase multiplied by 40%, the amount of the index gains that you are allowed), compared with 21%, if you opted for the maximum potential return (the 27.97% multiplied by 75% of the index gains). Of course without the guaranteed return you will earn nothing for the period if the S&P 500 stagnates or declines.

To open an account, you need to deposit at least $1,000, and it is federally insured up to $100,000. Although there are no fees or commissions involved, you will incur a substantial penalty withdrawing early. For example, if you withdraw a $10,000 1-year investment with three months still to go, you will get back only $9,850. If less than four weeks remained, you lose only the interest. With regular CDs, the early withdrawal penalty for those under one year is one month's interest and for those longer than one year, you lose three months' returns.

For savers who yearn for stock-market-like returns but are reluctant to assume the risk, taking the Chase Market Index Investment may be the way for them to get at least a taste of the stock market without any chance of principal loss.

As more banks follow Chase Manhattan's suit, it's inevitable that in the near future, all financial institutions will be offering much the same services and investments. This means still more options for the investor and you'll have to spend more time keeping up with what's happening, doing research, and seeking out the best deals.

No matter what you choose to put your money in, it inevitably involves accepting a certain amount of risk. What you invest in depends largely on what your goals are and whether these are short term or long term in scope.

When interest rates move up and down erratically, as they have been doing so often in recent years, this means prices have also been very volatile. This is because prices of fixed-income securities, such as bonds, move in the opposite direction to interest rates. When rates go up, prices come down, and vice versa. If you need to sell your securities during periods when prices are down sharply, you may sustain great losses. If your goal is for a low-risk profile, your best bet is to stay short, say a year or less.

Banks and thrifts

With deregulation and the recent spate of closings, banks and savings institutions are going through some tough times. How safe your bank is has become a most crucial question. Just being insured is not enough—who insures it is what makes the difference now.

"Only deposit your savings with a bank or thrift that is insured by one of the three federal insurance agencies—the Federal Deposit Insurance Corp., [FDIC], the Federal Savings & Loan Insurance Corp., [FSLIC], or the National Credit Union Share Insurance Fund," warns Glen King Parker, editor of *Income and Safety,* a newsletter based in Fort Lauderdale, FL. Note, in particular, the insurance covers accounts up to $100,000, which includes principal and interest.

The reason for this advice is that state-sponsored deposit insurance has proven worthless time and time again. Says Parker, "We cannot predict where or when the next run will occur, but we can predict that it will happen. Remember, in a bank run, the first person in line gets paid and the last one in line gets left out in the cold."

It should also be pointed out that not all federally insured institutions are healthy. In fact, by the summer of 1987, the FSLIC was on the verge of bankruptcy. The House and Senate pushed through a broad banking bill to provide the FSLIC with new funds so it can start bailing out sick thrifts in economically depressed states such as Texas and Oklahoma.

In competition with the financial centers, banks and thrifts today offer an assortment of savings accounts. With the passing of the traditional 5.50% passbook account, these institutions are now free to pay any rate they wish. As they do not have to advertise this fact, it's up to you to ask and shop around for the highest possible rate.

"The trend," says Robert Heady, publisher of *100 Highest Yields,* "is towards tier accounts, where your rate of interest is based on the size of your account—the bigger the balance, the higher the return." The result: existing accounts with check-writing privileges, such as NOWs (negotiable orders of withdrawal accounts), SuperNOWs, and money market accounts (MMAs) are increasingly being merged into tier accounts. With deregulation in full swing, you'll find it pays to shop around. Often the best rates may be from another state. For example, Texas has highly competitive institutions that continue to offer the nation's top yields in most categories of savings deposits. During periods of low interest rates, as in 1986, the highest yields are especially attractive, for they tend to pay about 20% or more than the national averages. Table 7.1 compares the highest yields in 1986 with the national averages of some common types of savings deposit.

TABLE 7.1

Type of Savings Deposit	National Average (%)	Highest Yield (%)
Money market accounts	5.44	6.96
6-month CDs	5.92	7.22
1-year CDs	6.17	7.49
2½-year CDs	6.61	7.79
5-year CDs	7.15	8.50

Note: As of year-end 1986.
Source: Bank Rate Monitor.

Opening an account in an out-of-state institution is really quite simple. With the record 125 banks closing in 1986, your first priority is to protect yourself by picking only those that are federally insured and stay within the $100,000 limit. When a federally insured institution fails, the federal agency involved moves in immediately. Despite some 400 federally insured bank failures in five years, no savers have lost a penny. Let's take a look at the FDIC. In 70% of its cases, the FDIC engineers an overnight merger with a healthier bank. For example, when the Heritage National Bank of Richardson, TX closed on September 25, 1986, its $30.1 million in deposits were transferred to a new unit of Dallas' Brookhollow National Bank. With larger institutions where a merger is not possible, the FDIC pays off the depositors, usually within two to five days, sometimes through an agent bank in the area.

How do you locate the high yielders? The financial section of your local newspaper may carry a weekly column on just this topic, as do the *Wall Street Journal, Barron's,* and *The New York Times.* There are newsletters, such as *100 Highest Yields,* and of course magazines, such as *Money* where a whole page in the section called Investor's Scorecard is devoted to the month's best rates in five different types of savings. Once you've found what you wanted, just call or write for information. Then conduct your banking by mail or by wire. When opening the account, be sure to make your check out to the institution, not to an individual.

Note: the hunt for safe high-yield savings will change dramatically now that the new banking bill, approved in June 1987 by House and Senate conferees, is law. As FSLIC starts to use the infusion of cash to bail out sick thrifts in economically depressed states, such as Texas, you will see fewer institutions offering extra high yields to attract funds, as many shaky S&Ls did in the recent past. What this means is you may no longer need to go out of state to find the best deals. You may find the higher yields being offered by your neighborhood bank or thrift.

Here's how high-yield depositors may be affected, when the FSLIC starts merging several weak thrifts to create a healthy entity:

- Your funds would remain fully insured up to $100,000. If you had an account in your name at thrift A and another at thrift B and together they total more than $100,000, after the merger the two accounts would remain separately insured (in their individual amounts) for six months or until the first of the two CDs matured, whichever time period was longer.

- The rate on your CD would not change, unless the Federal Home Loan Bank took the extraordinary step of closing all accounts and converting them to passbook accounts paying 5.5%. That's happened only a handful of times in the last two-and-a-half years. Beyond that, *100 Highest Yields* reported in a copyrighted June 29, 1987 story that it won't happen in Texas, because the FSLIC and Texas Savings and Loan League have agreed not to roll back rates in an effort to assure depositors so they will keep their funds in Texas.

- The rate on your MMA could fall if the acquiring institution pays lower rates. Since deregulation, institutions are free to change MMA yields at any time.

- Your uninsured deposits, that is, amounts above $100,000 in one name, may be transferred to the acquiring institution. But not always. If that happens, you will become a creditor of the old thrift and will have to wait in line for the payouts.

Once a merger has gone through, there's really nothing for you to do. You will receive a notice from the new institution that you are now its customer. You'll also be told of any changes in your account, and probably be given a telephone number or address in case you have queries.

In addition to checking accounts, banks and thrifts also offer an assortment of time deposit accounts, such as certificates of deposit (CDs)—all insured up to $100,000. These come in varying amounts and maturities that range from 1-month, 3-month, 6-month, 1-year, 1-1/2-year, 2-year, to 2-1/2-year and 5-year.

CDs are not for everyone since minimum deposits tend to get the lower returns. Initial minimum investments generally start at $1,000, but the more money you have, the more clout you can exert and the higher the interest rate. For example, CDs under $10,000 tend to pay rates less than U.S. Treasury securities; those of $10,000 or more are pegged to Treasury issues, while those of $100,000 or more—known as Jumbos—have negotiated interest rates. Opening a CD account is easy—just fill in an application form and pick a maturity date.

One thing to remember about CDs and time deposits in general: if you withdraw before the maturity date, you'll have to pay a rather substantial penalty. But because this penalty is tax deductible, at times you may find it advantageous to incur this loss.

Another pitfall is locking in at a lower rate over an extended period of time. So pick your maturity dates carefully. If you don't want to incur a penalty or to lose out on interest opportunities, then invest in CDs only with money you don't need in an emergency and pick a relatively short maturity date, for example, six months or a year. For some sample rates, please turn to Table 7.1.

Money market funds and money market investment accounts

Money market funds have become such a common part of our financial life today that it's hard to imagine the first fund was started only in 1972. In fact, in recent years it's become so successful that it's being copied by banks and other savings institutions, which now offer something called money market investment accounts.

Both money market funds and investment accounts invest only in short-term money-market instruments, such as U.S. Treasury bills—considered the safest instrument and thus best suited for conservative investors—or commercial paper and lower-rated corporations, which offer higher returns to compensate for higher risk.

There's another similarity between these two types of money market products: both are much like a savings account that also offers you check-writing privileges. You may deposit and withdraw your money as you wish. Your deposit earns an interest rate according to the types of securities the funds invest in.

Recently, both types of funds have been offering pretty comparable returns of around 6%. So the decision to choose one or the other fund depends more on your perception of safety—the bank funds are insured up to $100,000, while most of the regular money market funds are not. But it should be added that so far there have been no major defaults among money market funds that are open to individual investors.

To open a money market fund account, call the fund directly for a prospectus and an application. Some funds may require a minimum initial deposit of $1,000. For the money market investment accounts, banks may require not only a minimum initial deposit, which is often $1,000 or more, but also what's known as a maintenance balance. That is, if your average daily gross balance falls below that minimum, you'll incur a service charge. Also, if you exceed the three-check limit per month, you'll have to pay a hefty fee (say, $10) on each additional check that you have used. Money market funds don't impose such a minimum or charge a service fee, but some funds may require that your checks be for $500 or more.

For more on money market funds, please turn to chapter 8.

Strategies to deal with declining and rising rates

Rates go in cycles. For example, during early 1987, savings rates continued to dip lower, which followed a trend that started in August 1984. During 1986, the Federal Reserve Board trimmed its discount rate four times from 7.5% to 5.5%. From these reductions, a pattern has emerged. About 30 days after each of the half-point discount cuts, rates on money market accounts dropped a quarter of a point and CDs fell by a third of a point.

This same pattern can be applied to rising rates as well. For example, within three or four weeks after the Federal Reserve raised the discount rate to 6% from 5.5% in early September 1987, money market accounts rose a tenth of a point and CDs gained over a third of a point.

In a low-rate climate or during periods of transition, a safe bet is to park your cash in a high-yield money market account or in a 6-month CD. In general, money market accounts offer advantages over CDs. You get more liquidity plus check-writing privileges—usually with up to three checks per month free. The rate paid by money market accounts, however, can change at any time, whereas with CDs you are guaranteed the stated rate for the specified time period.

Economic factors that move interest rates

During early February 1987, interest rates continued to drift downward, with the long end falling more than the short. For example, the national average for 5-year CDs dropped to 7.12% from 7.15%, while 6-month CDs were down to 5.89% from 5.90%. This reflected bankers' expectations that rates would remain low, at least for the foreseeable future. When bankers start raising rates on the long end, it's a signal that the time may be ripe for the trend to move upward. Here are some major economic factors that influence the rise or fall of interest rates:

- The economy—rates tend to go up during a rising economy and down when it's sluggish, as it did during 1986.
- The dollar—just the opposite is true here. When the dollar is mighty, interest rates come down. But if the dollar stays weak, sooner or later rising inflation will push interest rates higher.
- The inflation rate—high inflation pushes up interest rates, while a low one depresses them. That is why rates have been so skimpy lately that savers are suffering, even after considering inflation. For example, since interest rates peaked in August 1984, the average yield for 1-year CDs has dropped to 6.14% from 11.65%, according to the *Bank Rate Monitor.* The annual inflation rate, however, as based on the consumer price index, dropped to 1.1% for 1986, the lowest increase in 25 years, versus

3.7% in 1984. That means savers today are getting real returns of only 5%, compared with 8% in 1984.

- Seasonal and demand factors—banks and thrifts must bid up deposit rates when they have to replace funds used for loans, such as home mortgages. Here, changes in the weather, and the start or end of a school year may play a part. For example, spring is usually the time when home buyers start looking for houses.

- Local competition—under the complete deregulation, local competition or the lack of it is becoming the determining factor in what pushes rates up or down. For example, in mid-January 1987, the five largest commercial banks in Los Angeles paid paltry yields of 4.65% to 4.80% on their lowest-tier accounts, while in Boston the big five were offering 5.25% to 5.70%.

By keeping an eye on the Bank Rate Monitor national averages that are published weekly in major newspapers, you'll have a barometer of where savings rates are heading. If rates are on the way up, it will start with the 5-year CDs. In addition, the high yielders usually lag behind the averages by about four weeks. However, the highest yields in some hot housing markets, such as Boston or Washington, D.C., may move ahead of the others.

The United States government

As the federal deficit continues to grow unabated, the United States government has become a major competitor for your savings dollars. You'll find the Treasury Department in the market almost any week selling some form of debt security with varying maturity dates. Those under a year are known as *Treasury bills* (T-bills). These short-term securities are issued with maturities of 3, 6, and 12 months. The intermediate-term issues, called *notes*, have maturities from two to ten years, while the long-term securities, the bonds, range from over 10 to 30 years.

All these securities carry the highest credit rating and are considered the direct obligation of the United States government. Best of all, the income you earn from these is exempt from state and local income taxes. So, if safety is your top priority, then you should certainly consider some Treasury securities in your portfolio.

The minimum initial investment for Treasury bills is $10,000, and in multiples of $5,000 after that. The initial minimum for notes with maturities of two and three years is $5,000; from 4 to 10 years, it is $1,000, which is also what's required for Treasury bonds. You may participate in the Treasury market even if you don't have this minimum; simply pick a money market fund that invests in these issues.

You may purchase the newly issued Treasury securities without any fees in person at the Bureau of Public Debt in Washington, D.C.; from any of the 36 Federal Reserve Banks and branches (for one nearest you, see Table 7.7); or by submitting a check with a letter, similar to the one in the next section. Check the financial news section of your newspaper or the *Wall Street Journal* for auction dates. These United States securities are also available from your local bank or broker, but they'll charge you a fee—often $20 to $30.

How to buy Treasury issues by mail.   Auctions for 3- and 6-month bills are usually held every Monday and 12-month bills every four weeks on Thursdays. Notes and bonds are sold at various times. If you submit a bid by mail, your letter must be postmarked by midnight the day before the auction, and received by the Federal Reserve Bank by 1 p.m. on the issue date.

If you are interested in submitting a bid, you may get a tender form from the Federal Reserve Bank nearest you, or you may send them a note, similar to the example here.

123 Main Street
Average City
Average State

October 21, 1987

Gentlemen:

This is my/our noncompetitive tender for a $10,000 Treasury bill of the new series, maturing in 3 months. At maturity, I'd/we'd like/not like the funds to be reinvested. Please mail it to me/us at the above address in registered form, made out to.... My social security number is xxx-xx-xxxx. Enclosed is a completed W-9 form and my/our certified check covering the cost of this bill.

Sincerely,

Enclosures

With this letter, enclose a certified check for the full face value of the security you're tendering for ($1,000, $5,000, or $10,000, for example). To ensure the Treasury will not withhold 20% of your interest earnings, you should also submit a signed W-9 form. Within a week or so, you'll be notified whether your bid has been accepted or not.

There are two ways to bid for Treasury securities: a competitive bid, a strategy used mainly by financial institutions or securities dealers, where you state the price you're prepared to pay. If it's too low, it will be automatically rejected; and a noncompetitive bid, which most individuals prefer, as the letter has done. By paying an average price, you are assured of getting something.

United States Savings Bonds.   One easy way to invest in the Federal government is by buying U.S. Savings Bonds, which are often available where you work under payroll deduction. Rates are set every six months and are generally comparable with the rest of the money market.

In the fall of 1986, the minimum annual interest rate on new issues dropped to 6% from 7.5%. This minimum rate applies to Series EE bonds that were issued from early November 1986, and are held for at least five years. Note, if market rates increase, the interest actually paid on the bonds may rise during their lifetime. The rate will be based on the higher of 6% or 85% of the average yield of outstanding Treasury notes and bonds with 5-year maturities.

With the drop in the minimum rate to 6%, the maturity (based on the time it takes a bond to double in value from its issue price to its face amount) of new savings bonds will increase to 12 years from 10.

For people with small amounts of money to save, buying U.S. Savings Bonds is a convenient and inexpensive way to invest. The minimum for Series EE bonds is only $25, compared with $1,000 or more for Treasury notes. However, you can earn more with the latter. For example, 5-year Treasury notes were recently quoted to yield about 6.75%, and 10-year notes, at 7.25%. Another added plus for the EE bonds is that they are exempt from state and local income taxes; the federal income tax on the accrued interest can be deferred until the bonds are cashed or mature.

The EE bonds have drawbacks as well. Because the minimum rate for the first five years after issuance is based on a sliding scale that starts well below 6%, if you need your money back earlier, you will end up with a much lower return. Also, if interest rates should trend upward again, you'd want to be in something more liquid than the EE bonds so you can take advantage of the rise.

Are zeros for you?   If you're saving for some specific goal that's in the future, say, retirement or for your children's college education, then you should check out zero bonds. These are typically Treasury securities—but they are also available in corporate and tax-exempt bonds—where the coupons (the semiannual interest payments) have been stripped from the principal payments. The two parts are then repackaged and sold with catchy names like CATS offered by Salomon Brothers, and TIGRS by Merrill Lynch.

With zeros, you get no regular interest payouts. Instead, you get a big discount on the price when you buy them, plus a fixed rate of return and a set value at maturity.

"Zeros are appealing because they often carry double-digit interest rates. Money is automatically compounded at a fixed, guaranteed rate for the life of the certificate," says Ned Costello of Fidelity Investments. "They're also relatively safe because they're backed by the full faith and credit of the United States government." However, the Federal government expects you to pay the taxes due on these bonds each year. As a result, zeros are ideal for tax-deferred accounts, such as IRAs. Parents in search of ways to finance their children's college education at a future date should check out tax-exempt zeros.

Offered in units of $1,000 of face value, the price of CATS, and zeros in general, is determined by the length of maturity—the longer out it goes, the lower the price. For example, a typical 5-year zero is roughly $680, a 10-year is $430, and a 20-year is $94. At maturity, you'll get the full $1,000.

Fannie and Ginnie Maes.   In recent years, individual investors have been snapping up mortgage-backed securities issued by three United States federal agencies and available through your brokers.

Fannie Maes are issued by the Federal National Mortgage Association, a government-sponsored corporation owned entirely by private shareholders. They come in varying maturities and in amounts of $10,000, $25,000, $50,000, $100,000, and $500,000. Proceeds are used to buy Federal Housing Administration, Veterans Administration, or Farmers Home Administration insured or guaranteed mortgages.

Ginnie Maes are mortgage-backed securities guaranteed by the Government National Mortgage Association. What this really means is that these guarantees are backed by the full faith and credit of the United States government. Although Ginnie Maes come in multiples of $5,000, your initial investment has to be $25,000. As of June 1987, Ginnie Maes have $290 billion outstanding. Because of the size of this market, Ginnie Maes enjoy a high degree of liquidity. This, plus government support, has helped to make Ginnie Maes popular with mutual funds, thrifts, trusts, and pension funds.

Freddie Mac, the Federal Home Loan Mortgage Corporation, was set up as a profit-making part of the 12 Federal Home Loan banks, to increase the availability of mortgage credit by turning conventional mortgages into bond-like securities. By pooling the mortgages it buys from originating banks and thrifts, Freddie Mac then adds its own guarantee. Freddie Mac backs these by the full faith and credit of the United States government then adds a quarter of a point for expenses and profit and sells the pools to long-term investors.

Unlike Treasury bills, notes, or bonds, these mortgage securities are subject to federal, state, and local income taxes. If you're considering a long-term investment that also provides you a monthly income—the paybacks include interest and part return of principal—then you should check out these mortgage-backed securities.

Corporations: bonds and debentures

Just as an individual can go to a bank and take out a loan for home improvement or for education, so can a corporation when it needs cash for expansion. But instead of borrowing from a bank, the company may float a bond issue and get investors like yourself to invest in it. In return for the use of your money, the company promises to pay you an annual fixed interest return, plus the principal at a set maturity date. Bonds are considered senior securities, which means that in case of default, the company must first pay off its bondholders, even before its shareholders.

Companies may also issue debentures, which are junior to bonds but are otherwise similar.

At one time bonds were considered one of the safest investments. In the 1970s, this changed when interest rates and inflation ran rampant and the bond markets fell into chaos. Investors who traded suffered great losses—as interest rates shot up, bond prices tumbled to new lows. Even those lucky enough to lock up high returns found they were also losing as super inflation was gobbling up their gains.

Bondholders are now seeing a nice return on their investment because inflation has abated. But be aware that if you have locked up some high rates, you may lose them since they can be called away from you or you can be refunded with lower-paying instruments. This happens because companies that had borrowed when rates were high would want to refinance their debt when rates are down—much like you would with your mortgage. When you buy a bond, make sure you check the call protection clause—typically, you get five years before an issue can be called or refunded.

Bonds, with face amounts of $1,000 or $5,000, are available from brokers. For most small investors, the best way to invest in bonds is to get into one of the bond mutual funds. In addition to saving on commission, you also get expert management and a ready-made diversified portfolio.

States and local municipalities: tax-exempt/municipal bonds

While most bonds offered by companies are taxable, those offered by state and local municipalities are usually tax exempt.

Tax-exempt bonds come in $5,000 denominations. Buying one bond makes little sense though since you'll have a hard time buying and selling it—not to mention the high brokerage commission you'll be paying if they'll bother with you at all.

You can participate in the tax-exempt market without having to buy your own bonds. One easy way is to get a bond fund or money market fund that invests in tax-exempt issues. Or you may look into unit trusts that invest in municipal bonds. A trust is basically a fund with a set portfolio that requires no managing; once it is subscribed, it will take no more new investors. John Nuveen and Merrill Lynch are two of the major players in this area.

Munis are tax exempt from federal, state, and local taxes if you own bonds issued by an entity in the same state where you are a resident. You get the maximum benefit if you are a high-tax-bracket person—say 38.5%. This becomes clear when you see how the taxable equivalent yield is calculated:

$$\frac{\text{Tax-exempt yields}}{100\% \text{ minus your tax bracket}} = \text{your taxable equivalent yield}$$

If you're in the 15% tax bracket and the tax-exempt issue yields 7.50%, then your taxable equivalent yield will be 8.8%. However, if you're in the 38.5% bracket, then the equivalent becomes 12.2%. Table 7.2 shows at a glance how much various tax-exempt yields are worth in the five 1987 tax brackets.

TABLE 7.2   Taxable equivalent yields at a glance

Tax-Exempt Yields*	1987 Tax Bracket				
	11%	15%	28%	35%	38.5%
3.00	3.37	3.52	4.16	4.61	4.87
3.50	3.93	4.12	4.86	5.38	5.69
4.00	4.49	4.71	5.56	6.15	6.50
4.50	5.06	5.29	6.25	6.92	7.32
5.00	5.62	5.88	6.94	7.69	8.13
5.50	6.18	6.47	7.64	8.46	8.94
6.00	6.74	7.06	8.33	9.23	9.76
6.50	7.30	7.65	9.03	10.00	10.57
7.00	7.87	8.24	9.72	10.77	11.38
7.50	8.43	8.82	10.42	11.54	12.20
8.00	8.99	9.41	11.11	12.31	13.01
8.50	9.55	10.00	11.81	13.08	13.82
9.00	10.11	10.59	12.50	13.85	14.63
9.50	10.67	11.17	13.19	14.61	15.44
10.00	11.23	11.76	13.88	15.38	16.26

*All numbers in the table are percentages.

For tax rate tables, please turn to Chapter 4.

Table 7.3 is a summary of the many ways to invest for income.

TABLE 7.3

Type (Maturities)	Offered by/ (Available from)	Recent Yields (%)	Minimum Investment ($)	Comments
NOWs	Banks, S&Ls Credit unions	5.00	2,500	Insured up to $100,000
SuperNOWs	Banks, S&Ls Credit Unions	5.50	2,500	Insured up to $100,000
Money market accounts	Banks, S&Ls	5.50	1,000	Insured up to $100,000
Money market funds	Investment companies	5.50	100	Free checking
CDs (3 months to 7 years)	Banks, S&Ls Credit unions	7.00 to 9.00	1,000	Insured up to $100,000
Bills (3 to 6 months)	U.S. Treasury (Federal Reserve, banks/brokers)	6.50 to 7.00	10,000	Highest rating
Notes (2 and 3 years) (4 to 10 years)		8.41 to 8.75	5,000 1,000	
Bonds (10 to 30 years)		9.56 to 9.72	1,000	
U.S. Savings Bonds	U.S.	6.00	25 and up	Convenient for small investors
Zeros/strips	U.S. Treasury/ corporate/ tax-exempt (brokers/funds)	8.08 to 10.11	250 and up	Good for some future goal
Mortgage-backed securities	Ginnie Maes Fannie Maes Freddie Macs	9.00 to 11.00	25,000 10,000	One way to be in real estate
Bonds (10 to 30 years)	Corporations	10.00 to 11.50	5,000	Can be volatile
	States and local muni-cipalities (brokers/funds)	5.50 to 8.50	5,000	Tax-free income can be tempting

INVESTING FOR GROWTH: STOCKS

When a corporation needs money for expansion, it may make a private placement with a bank, or it may have a public offering of stocks. When you buy the common stock of a company, in effect you become an owner of the firm. As a member of the family, you will enjoy both the good and the bad fortunes of the company. If it makes money you share in the profits, but if it loses you will be poorer.

Publicly owned companies are listed on one of the stock exchanges. The major exchanges are the New York Stock Exchange (NYSE)—often called the Big Board—with about 1700 listed stocks; the American Stock Exchange (AMEX) has about 900; and the NASDAQ over-the-counter (OTC) has about 6000 and is growing daily.

You'll find good and bad companies in all the exchanges. Broadly speaking, the older, larger companies are on the Big Board. For example, all 30 stocks included in the Dow Jones Industrial Average, a commonly used indicator of how the market is doing, are listed on the New York Stock Exchange. The newer and smaller ones are on the over-the-counter (OTC). Just as an elderly person is less active than a young child, so it is with companies. The more seasoned stocks—the more mature ones are often called "blue chips"—tend to be less volatile, command a higher price, and pay shareholders a dividend. However, the new issues may fluctuate more in price, cost less to buy, pay no dividends, but may have greater potential for growth. Penny stocks, shares that cost under $1, tend to be the most volatile of all.

In addition to the Dow Jones Industrial Average, there are other broader indicators that you can use to keep track of the market. The more common ones are the Standard & Poor's 500, the Value Line Composite (covering some 1700 companies), and the Wilshire 5000. Major exchanges, such as NYSE, AMEX, and NASDAQ-OTC, also have their own market indices. As each index is composed of varying numbers of companies, and frequently different types of industries, it follows that the results from them may also differ. Table 7.4 gives some idea of how these indices performed in 1986.

TABLE 7.4

Index	1986 % Gain	Comments
Dow Jones Industrial	22.58	30 Blue Chips, all on NYSE
Standard & Poor's 500	14.62	500 mostly from NYSE
New York Stock Exchange	13.98	1700 big-cap companies
Wilshire 5000	12.48	5000, including all NYSE, some AMEX and OTC
NASDAQ over-the-counter	7.36	6000, mostly newer and smaller-cap companies
American Stock Exchange	6.96	900, including a large number of smaller oil exploration/drilling companies
Value Line Composite	5.01	1700 mostly from NYSE, some AMEX and OTC

A closer look at the Dow 30 in Table 7.5 shows that the blue-chip rally of 1986 really benefited only a select few. For example, only a dozen companies posted price increases of 20% or more for the year, and nine actually had decreases up to 60%. The lackluster performers included two bellwethers: AT&T, whose shares ended at $25 a share, unchanged for the year; and General Motors, down 6.2% to $66 in 12 months.

Note, although the Dow 30 had a banner year in 1986, the secondary issues on the AMEX and the NASDAQ-OTC started showing signs of new life in early 1987. According to some experts, the time may be ripe for some of these issues to take off, but nine months into the year, the Dow 30 are still leading, gaining 36.9% during that period.

Table 7.6 is a summary of the broad categories of common stocks, based on risk in ascending order, on the market today.

TABLE 7.5 The Dow 30

Company	1986 Percent Gain (or loss)	Price ($) 12/31/86	Price ($) 9/30/87	Earnings or Loss per Share		
				Actual 9/86	Estimated 1987	Estimated 1988
Owens-Illinois*	100.91	53.00	N.A.	N.A.	N.A.	N.A.
Merck	80.85	123.88	206.88	4.85	6.38	7.76
Philip Morris	62.66	71.88	118.88	6.12	7.82	9.75
International Paper	48.04	37.56	51.88	2.89	3.40	4.34
Primerica (American Can)	40.22	42.06	45.00	3.65	3.70	4.31
Eastman Kodak	35.55	68.75	101.88	3.41	5.21	6.18
Goodyear Tire	34.02	42.00	71.63	2.74	6.28	7.63
3M	29.95	58.38	81.75	3.40	3.94	4.46
F. W. Woolworth	28.77	38.75	49.25	3.30	3.85	4.43
Exxon	27.21	35.06	48.63	3.70	3.29	3.61
Westinghouse Electric	25.28	55.88	73.25	4.42	5.19	5.79
Dupont	23.75	84.00	119.13	6.35	7.28	8.18
Texaco	19.60	36.00	40.50	3.01	3.08	3.71
Chevron	19.01	45.38	53.88	2.01	3.08	3.76
General Electric	18.21	43.00	61.50	2.73	3.19	3.69
McDonald's	12.87	40.67	54.00	2.49	2.91	3.44
Procter & Gamble	9.51	76.38	101.00	4.60	5.77	6.39
American Express	6.85	28.38	35.88	2.25	2.03	3.16
United Technologies	5.14	46.00	58.00	0.13	4.43	5.29
Sears Roebuck	1.92	39.88	51.88	3.62	4.43	5.03
AT&T	0.00	25.00	33.75	0.21	1.77	2.07
Allied-Signal	-4.59	40.13	45.63	3.31	3.07	3.41
Union Carbide	-4.62	22.63	28.25	1.26	2.21	2.77
General Motors	-6.22	66.00	83.00	8.55	8.01	9.10
Inco*	-11.32	11.75	N.A.	N.A.	N.A.	N.A.

TABLE 7.5 (Cont.)

Company	1986 Percent Gain (or loss)	Price ($) 12/31/86	Price ($) 9/30/87	Earnings or Loss per Share Actual 9/86	Estimated 1987	Estimated 1988
Aluminum Co. of America	−12.00	34.00	61.63	2.96	3.27	4.79
USX Corp.	−19.26	21.63	37.25	−6.74	1.21	2.96
IBM	−22.83	120.00	150.75	7.81	8.93	10.91
Navistar International	−44.12	4.88	7.25	−0.18	0.55	0.92
Bethlehem Steel	−60.01	6.25	17.63	−3.70	1.04	2.10
Boeing†	N.A.	51.13	50.88	4.28	3.06	3.69
Coca Cola†	N.A.	37.88	48.38	1.91	2.41	2.77

Notes: Prices have been adjusted for splits. Changes in 1987. * removed from list; † added to list. N.A. = not applicable.

Source: Zacks Investment Research Inc.

TABLE 7.6

Type	Major Variables
Blue chips	High price, high income
Matured-company	Good income, with some growth
Growth company	Little income, good gains potential
Special situation	Can be any on this list with something special going on that make them attractive
New issues	New public companies, volatile
Penny stocks	Under $1, developing firms, very volatile

INVESTING FOR SELF/ASSET PRESERVATION

The rapid changes in recent years in both the economic climate and tax laws mean investors have been inundated with new investment products or strategies that are supposed to meet their every contingency. The most common of these strategies are

- Hedging by trading futures or options, where experienced traders may be able to hedge their bets on the stock market by buying *calls,* the right to buy 100 shares of stock at a certain price, and *puts,* the right to sell 100 shares at a certain price. True hedgers will buy both calls and puts to "cover" themselves so that no matter whether the underlying stock goes up or down, they'll win. The main difference is they will trade more calls in an up-market, but will revert to more puts, when the going is bad.

- Sheltering your income by seeking out tax-advantaged investments. This strategy requires one element: the higher the income, the greater the benefit. There are basically two types of tax-advantaged investments: 1) those that allow you to take writeoffs, that is, you simply write it off; and 2) tax-deferred, such as in an annuity, where you'll pay the taxes on it at a future date, when you'll hopefully be in a lower tax bracket.

There are three elements common to all tax shelters—tax benefits, cash flow, and appreciation. In the decade before the Reagan era, the Federal government favored tax benefits, so most programs on the markets were generous with deductions and writeoffs.

Starting with the 1984 Tax Reform Act, some of the tax benefits were cut back. The remaining tax benefits were further reduced by the 1986 Tax Reform Act. This means the other two elements would have to take higher priority.

The 1984 Act included a number of measures designed to tighten up on perceived tax shelter abuses. One provision prohibits investors from taking deductions against expenses that will be incurred in the future. If you invest in tax shelters, pay special care to programs such as oil and gas drilling, research and development, and cattle-feeding programs, where deductions are often based on prepaid expenses. Another provision increases the period over which real property may be depreciated to 18 years from 15 years.

With the passage of the Tax Reform Act of 1986, the screws on tax shelters were tightened further. By dropping the top bracket rate to 28% from 50%, some experts say there will be even less need for tax shelters in the future.

For more details on the new bill, including tax-bracket tables, please turn to Chapter 4.

- Inflation hedges—during the 1970s, when inflation rates were at double digits, investors found hard assets (gold and diamonds) or collectibles (art, stamps, and coins) ideal inflation hedges. Some of these items skyrocketed to such unrealistically high levels that people who bought at those record prices have suffered steep losses.

  Let's take a look at the diamond prices in Table 7.7. Between 1975 and 1980, prices of an investment-grade D-flawless one-carat stone rose to over $62,000 from $4,000. Then prices started to drop steadily for the next few years to about $9,000 in 1986. Since then, it's been on an upward curve and dealers are expecting brighter days ahead.

  Note that the better jewelry-grade diamonds have been pretty steady through the years and are appreciating nicely.

TABLE 7.7 Precious gems: diamond prices are never forever

One carat gems	1987 (June), ($)	1986 Price ($)	1985 Price ($)	1980 Price ($)	1975 Price ($)
Diamond					
D–flawless/brilliant cut (top investment grade)	13,000–15,675	9,500–12,000	14,000–18,000	55,000–62,000	4,000–5,000
GHI–VS/brilliant cut (white jewelry stone with a very slight inclusion)	3,000–3,500	2,200–2,450	2,200–2,300	2,700–3,000	850–925
Full cuts: .02 to .15 carats (small stones for rings, bracelets, watches, pendants)	390–410	380–400	380–400	400–440	175–220
Fancy cuts					
GHI–VS marquise	2,950–3,250	2,530–2,818	2,530–2,645	3,163–3,450	978–1,064
D–flawless marquise	7,500–8,500	6,000–7,000	8,400–10,800	33,000–37,200	2,400–3,000
GHI–VS emerald	2,250–2,550	1,980–2,205	1,980–2,205	2,475–2,700	765–833
D–flawless emerald	6,000–7,000	5,000–6,000	7,000–9,000	27,500–31,000	2,000–2,500

TABLE 7.7 (Cont.)

Emerald/emerald cut (deep emerald green preferably from Colombia rather than Zambia)	500–5,800	300–5,000	360–6,750	500–8,000	144–2,400
Ruby/faceted oval or cabochon (ruby red or pigeon's blood preferably from Burma)	600–6,800	600–6,000	720–4,800	1,050–7,780	288–1,920
Sapphire/faceted oval or antique cut (cornflower blue preferably from Kashmir, which is very hard to find; Burma)	400–4,000	300–3,500	600–4,320	400–4,000	288–1,560

Sources: The Diamond Registry and The Gemstone Registry, 30 West 47th Street, New York, N.Y. 10036; (212) 575-0444.

With inflation currently hovering around 5%, most people feel they have little need for inflation hedges. But if you think inflation will go up again, then you may want to follow what many investment advisers suggest: any well-designed investment portfolio should have 5% to 10% in gold, as a hedge against inflation. Table 7.8 lists some of the many ways to achieve that goal.

TABLE 7.8   The many ways to buy gold

Type	Comments
Physical	
Bullion	Tends to be very volatile in prices. Requires storage and you may have to pay an assay fee when you sell.
Coins	Also require storage but easily portable. Best to avoid the South African Krugerrand and get instead the American Eagle, the Australian Nugget, the Canadian Maple Leaf, or the Chinese Panda.
Certificates	No problem with storage since the gold doesn't change hands, but make sure you're dealing with a trustworthy firm.
Securities	
Stocks	Until recent years, the South African shares were popular with investors. Tend to be less volatile, and the attractive dividends they pay help to cushion any possible losses.
Mutual funds	More volatile than the diversified funds. An easy way to invest in gold. Most funds carry an 8.5% load.
Futures and options	Futures on commodities or options; can be rather volatile; options can also be done on your own shares, a hedging technique used by experienced traders to reduce losses.

The gold bugs—the purists—will tell you there's no other way to buy gold but in the physical form, that is, in bullion or bars. But in fact, there are at least six different ways to invest in this precious metal. As Table 7.8 shows, there's no one perfect way. With each method, you'll find both advantages and disadvantages.

For example, you can get gold as certificates or coins in addition to bullion. With bullion and coins you have to consider the question of storage: where are you going to keep it? If you have to rent a safety deposit box, even the smallest one will cost you about $25 a year. In addition to paying a broker's commission when you buy or sell, you also have to pay the shipping costs, and sometimes an assay fee when you sell if it's necessary to test the bars to make sure they are unadulterated. Don't forget, if you live in a state or locality with sales taxes—especially in high-priced spots such as New York City, which levies an 8.25% sales tax—that can also add substantially to your overall costs.

With the certificates you don't have a storage problem since the dealer who issues the certificates will safeguard it for you. But make sure you know that the person you're dealing with is trustworthy.

As long as the current unstable political situation in South Africa persists, it's best to stay away from the Krugerrands, a gold coin much favored by investors in recent years. Until recently advisers were promoting the Canadian Maple Leaf or the Chinese Panda, which are one ounce in weight. The price of the coins is based on the bullion, plus a 6% premium when you buy and a 2% premium when you sell. This is about what the Krugerrand used to command; now it's generally sold at a discount of about 3%.

There is now an American alternative: late in 1986, the U.S. Mint introduced the Eagle, which comes in four sizes—one ounce, half ounce, quarter ounce, and tenth of an ounce. The Eagles were such a success they sold out quickly and commanded premiums of as much as 30% for the smallest coins. Prices have since stabilized and the Eagles are trading at premiums similar to other comparable coins.

In May 1987, Australia launched its gold coin program in the United States. There are four Australian Nuggets weighing one ounce, half ounce, quarter ounce, and tenth of an ounce.

As securities, gold is available in common stock or as a commodity in the futures market. You can also write options on it—either in the futures market or on the shares that you own. Experienced traders use this as a hedging technique to cut their losses. For example, if you own shares in ASA, a closed-end fund listed on the New York Stock Exchange, and you perceive the market will be trending upwards, you write a *call* on your shares. However, if you think the market is on the way down, then you'll write a *put* instead. Either way, you'll be covered.

Until recently, the South African mining shares were popular with investors. These tend to be less volatile than the bullion, and the attractive returns or dividends—often 8% or more—help to cushion any possible losses.

For investors who don't want to be bothered with picking their own stocks, they can invest in gold funds. These tend to be more volatile than the diversified funds, and often move separately from the rest of the market, as you'll see in Table 7.9 of the four gold funds that have 10-year records.

TABLE 7.9   Gold funds: rates of return with income

| Name of Fund/ Telephone | Assets (millions, $) | Load (%) | Annualized | | |
			12/76– 12/86 (%)	12/81– 12/86 (%)	12/85– 12/86 (%)
International Investors (212) 687-5200	865	8.5	+24.5	+11.0	+34.2
Franklin Gold Fund (415) 570-3000	126	8.5	+21.8	+ 6.8	+30.7
United Services Gold Shares (800) 531-5777	307	No	+21.1	+ 4.0	+37.5
Strategic Investments (800) 527-5027	96	8.5	+19.0	− 0.2	+28.3
Standard & Poor's 500			+13.8	+19.8	+18.6
Salomon Bros. Corporate Bonds			+ 9.9	+22.5	+19.8

Source: CDA Investment Technologies, Silver Spring, MD 20902.

Which method you'll pick to invest in gold depends on your own philosophy and psychology. Some advisers suggest using more than one method as a way of diversifying. Another strategy to cut risk is to average in and average out, that is, buy and sell over a period of time so that the final price you pay will be averaged out over several transactions. For example, in a 10-month period, if you purchase gold once a month, at prices ranging from $200 to $400, your average price would be somewhere between those amounts.

TAKING THE NEXT STEP: WHERE TO GET HELP

Whether it's for assistance or information, Table 7.10 will help you get started.

TABLE 7.10   Where to get help

Source	What's Available
BANKING/MONEY MARKETS	
Comptroller of the Currency Office of Consumer Affairs 490 L'Enfant Plaza S.W. Washington, D.C. 20219 (202) 447-1600	Handles consumer complaints about banks with "national" or N.A. (national association) in their names.
The Donoghue Organization Box 540 Holliston, MA 01748 (617) 429-5930	A weekly, *Money Fund Report*, and a bimonthly, *Money-Letter*, which includes *Fund-Letter*, and *Donoghue's Mutual Funds Almanac*.
Federal Deposit Insurance Corporation Office of Consumer Affairs 550 17th Street N.W. Washington, D.C. 20429 (202) 393-8400	Regulates the federally insured state banks and can help with information and complaints about them.
Federal Home Loan Bank Board Office of the Secretary 1700 G Street, N.W. Washington, D.C. 20552 (202) 377-6000	Parent for the Federal Savings & Loan Insurance Corp. (FSLIC) regulates the federally chartered thrifts and deals with complaints about them.
Federal Reserve Board Division of Consumer Affairs 21st and C Streets N.W. Washington, D.C. 20551 (202) 452-2946	For complaints against state chartered banks, members of the Federal Reserve System. The 12 districts include Atlanta, Boston, Chicago, Cleveland, Dallas, Kansas City, Minneapolis, New York City, Philadelphia, Richmond, St. Louis, and San Francisco. You can save on brokerage fees by buying new Treasury issues at these district banks on days when they are being auctioned.

TABLE 7.10 *(Cont.)*

Source	What's Available
100 Highest Yields P. O. Box 088888 N. Palm Beach, FL 33408 (800) 327-7717	A weekly survey of federally insured institutions that are currently offering the highest yields. ($84 for 52 issues, or $19 for 6 trial issues; Visa or MasterCard accepted.)
COLLECTIBLES	
Appraisers Association of America 60 East 42nd street New York, NY 10165 (212) 867-9775	A list of appraisers including their specialities. To ensure against being over- or underinsured, it's a good idea to have all valuables properly appraised.
Christie's 502 Park Avenue New York, NY 10022 (212) 546-1000 and Sotheby's 1334 York Avenue New York, NY 10021 (212) 606-7000	Free evaluation services from the two leading names in the art and antique auction business. Simply call for an appointment with a specialist, or write and enclose a photograph of the work that you want evaluated.
Coin World or Linn's Stamp News P.O. Box 150 Sidney, OH 45365 (513) 498-2111	Whether you collect coins or stamps, one of these weeklies will keep you up-to-date with what's new. Price of *Coin World* is $26, and *Linn's Stamp News* is $22.95 for a year's subscription.
The Diamond Registry The Gemstone Registry 30 West 47th Street New York, NY 10036 (212) 565-0445	Computerized service for precious gem prices. A monthly newsletter is available at $90 ($100 overseas)/year for the 12 issues.
The Photograph Collector 127 East 59th Street New York, NY 10022 (212) 838-8640	A monthly newsletter covering the art of collecting photographs. ($90 for 12 issues.)
R.M. Smythe & Co. 24 Broadway New York, NY 10004 (212) 943-1880	The old domestic or foreign stock or bond certificates, antique coins or paper currencies sitting in your attic may actually be worth money. For a $25 appraisal fee, Smythe will give you the whole story. If you decide to sell, Smythe may even auction it for you.

TABLE 7.10 *(Cont.)*

Source	What's Available

CREDIT UNIONS

Credit Union National Association
Public Relations Department
P.O. Box 431
Madison, WI 53701
(608) 231-4000

Information about both state and federal credit unions, including what they are, how to organize one, or where to find one near you.

National Credit Union Administration
Office of Public Information
1776 G Street N.W.
Washington, D.C. 20456
(202) 357-1050

Parent for the National Credit Union Share Insurance Fund, with regional offices located in Atlanta, Austin, Boston, Chicago, Walnut Creek, CA, and Washington, D.C. This organization regulates federally chartered credit unions and assists in organizing a group or affiliating with an existing one.

FUTURES

Chicago Board of Trade
Office of Investigation and Audit
La Salle Street at Jackson Boulevard
Chicago, IL 60604
(312) 435-3500

Assistance with complaints against brokers who are members of the board; or if you're seeking monetary adjustment, you also can use its arbitration service. The board trades options on futures and futures contracts on four commodity groups: the grains, precious metals, financial instruments, and energy.

Chicago Mercantile Exchange
30 S. Wacker Drive
Chicago, IL 60606
(312) 930-1000

For arbitration or advice on trading foreign currencies, short-term interest rates, stock indexes, gold, lumber, and livestock. For market information, call (312) 930-8282.

Commodity Exchange Inc.
Public Relations Department
4 World Trade Center
New York, NY 10048
(212) 938-2000

Trades in gold, silver, copper and aluminum futures, plus options on gold futures. A list of Comex member firms, and brochures on the ins-and-outs of commodity trading is available.

Commodity Futures Trading
  Commission
2033 K Street N.W.
Washington, D.C. 20581

Regulates the futures industry. Works closely with the National Futures Association, a trade group (see next major entry).

  Enforcement:
  (202) 254-7424

Handles complaints about frauds, unauthorized trading, or other shady practices.

TABLE 7.10 *(Cont.)*

Source	What's Available
Information: (202) 254-9703	To check whether a firm or an individual is registered with the commission.
Complaints: Director of Complaints 2000 L St. N.W. Washington, D.C. 20581 (202) 254-6790	For reparation, or to find out if the commission or another customer has filed complaints.
National Futures Association Arbitration Administration 200 W. Madison Street Chicago, IL 60606 (312) 781-1300	Audits members to ensure they are in compliance with NFA standards. Helps to resolve disputes on futures and options transactions involving members.

GOLD

Source	What's Available
The Complete Book of Gold Investing by Jeffrey A. Nichols (Dow Jones-Irwin, 1987, $24.95)	A practical guide to help you better understand the workings of the gold market and how you can benefit from it.

SECURITIES

National Association of Securities
  Dealers

Source	What's Available
Arbitration Department 2 World Trade Center, 98th floor New York, NY 10048 (212) 839-6244	For legal action, contact the New York office, which handles all arbitrations.
Customer Complaint Department 1735 K Street N.W. Washington, D.C. 20006 (202) 728-8000	For complaints or other queries you have to get in touch with one of the 13 district offices. Call Washington for the one nearest you.
Securities and Exchange Commission Office of Consumer Affairs and Information Services 450 Fifth Street, N.W. Washington, D.C. 20549 (202) 272-7440	For complaints about brokers, exchanges or corporate issuers of stocks and bonds. All corporate filings with the SEC are available at the public reference libraries the commission operates in Washington D.C., New York City, and Chicago. For a small charge, copies are available on written request.
Securities Investor Protection Corp. 900 17th Street N.W. Washington, D.C. 20006 (202) 223-8400	Established by the federal government to cover certain investors' losses if a broker–dealer firm goes bankrupt. SIPC raises funds mainly by assessing the securities firms.

TABLE 7.10 *(Cont.)*

Source	What's Available

STOCK EXCHANGES

American Stock Exchange
Rulings and Inquiries Department
86 Trinity Place
New York, NY 10006
(212) 306-1000

For any information about the stocks traded on the exchange, or complaints about its member brokers. Among publications available, an annual statistical review of the exchange ($3).

Chicago Board of Options Exchange
Communications Department
LaSalle and Van Buren Streets
Chicago, IL 60605
(312) 786-7492

For general information on how to trade options.

New York Stock Exchange
11 Wall Street
New York, NY 10005
(212) 623-3000

For general information, get in touch with the communications division. For problems with brokers, seek help from the arbitration department. For any printed material on how to invest, write the publications department.

STOCK NEWSLETTERS/ PUBLICATIONS

Growth Stock Outlook
P. O. Box 15381
Chevy Chase, MD 20815
(301) 654-5205

A monthly newsletter covering growth stocks, available by subscription ($175 a year or $320 for two years).

Institute of Econometric Research
3471 N. Federal Highway
Fort Lauderdale, FL 33306
(305) 563-9000

Publishes the following:
- *Market Logic*—a general stock market advisory
- *The Insiders*—a record of what corporate insiders are doing
- *New Issues*—a guide to initial public offerings
- *Mutual Fund Forecaster*—with recommendations, profit projections and risk ratings
- *Income & Safety*—the many ways to invest for income, including money market funds

LaLoggia's Special Situation Report and Stock Market Forecast
P.O. Box 167
Rochester, NY 14601
(716) 232-1240

List of takeover candidates, updates, and ideas. Published every two to three weeks, depending on market conditions ($230 a year).

TABLE 7.10 *(Cont.)*

Source	What's Available
Select Information Exchange 2095 Broadway New York, NY 10023 (212) 874-6408	A subscription agency for more than 700 financial newsletters, SIE offers sampler packages for short trials. The basic package includes 20 newsletters of your choice for $11.95.
Standard & Poor's Corp. 25 Broadway New York, NY 10004 (212) 208-8000	Among a variety of basic reference publications for investors, S&P has the *Security Owner's Stock Guide* ($72/year), and the *Outlook* ($185/year).
1988 Stock Trader's Almanac The Hirsch Organization 6 Deer Trail Old Tappan, NJ 07675 (201) 664-3400	This little annual volume will keep track of your dates, social and business, as well as your investments, and arm you with enough data to gain, if not real profits, at least some insights into the stock trading game. ($21.95, plus $2.50 for postage and handling.) Also publishes two newsletters: *Smart Money*, a monthly covering America's undiscovered stocks ($98 a year, includes the *Stock Trader's Almanac*), and *Ground Floor*, a semimonthly on new technology issues ($115 a year).
The Bowser Report P. O. Box 6278 Newport News, VA 23606 (804) 877-5979	A monthly devoted to mini-priced stocks—those under $3 ($39/year).
The National OTC Stock Journal P.O. Box 24327 Denver, CO 80222 (303) 758-9131	The over-the-counter and new-issues market. Weekly ($79/49 issues); monthly ($29/12 issues).
Value Line 711 Third Avenue New York, NY 10017 (212) 687-3965	Value Line's three-part weekly *Investment Survey* includes stock selections, commentary on the stock market outlook, and fundamental statistics on some 1700 companies ($395 a year). Both *Value Line* and S&P publications are often available at your broker's office or at your local public library.

TABLE 7.10 *(Cont.)*

Source	What's Available
TREASURY SECURITIES	
Department of the Treasury Bureau of the Public Debt Washington, D.C. 20239 (202) 287-4113	Address here all queries on Treasury bills, notes, and bonds, that your local bank or Federal Reserve Bank or one of its branches can't answer. Also available here are brochures on the various Treasury securities.
U.S. SAVINGS BONDS	
Department of the Treasury Savings Bonds Division (Dept. PT) Washington, D.C. 20226 (800) US BONDS (202) USA-8888 or Bureau of Public Debt (304) 420-6112	For general information or questions about such problems as replacing lost bonds. It's best to check with your local bank first. The toll-free line gives the current rate. For more serious problems, call the Bureau of Public Debt.

Note: See Chapter 1, Table 1.2 for additional financial sources.

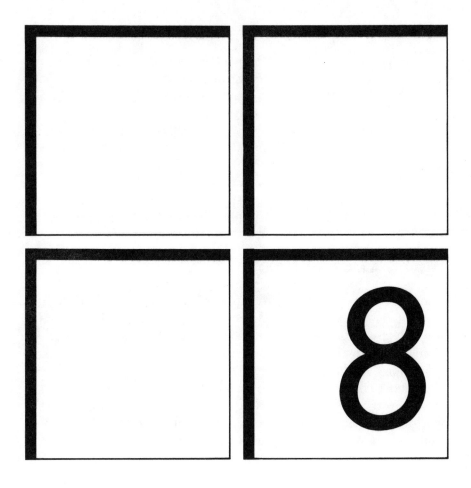

8

Mutual Funds

Although mutual funds have been around in this country for some 60 years, it's only in the last decade or so that there's been a phenomenal growth both in volume and in the types of funds available. Today, record numbers of Americans are investing in mutual funds. According to the Investment Company Institute, some 25 million shareholders with 50 million accounts have almost $750 billion invested in more than 2000 funds. For three years in a row the sales of stock, bond, and income funds reached new heights: in 1986 a record $211 billion, nearly double the $114 billion established in 1985, and more than four times the $45.9 billion set just two years earlier.

WHAT IS A MUTUAL FUND?

The concept of mutual funds is simple. Small investors don't have the clout of those with big money, who can afford top managers and a properly diversified portfolio. But if many people of modest means and similar goals pooled their money, they, too, could afford the best. A fund allows you to invest a relatively small amount of money, say $500, and get both diversification and professional management at lower cost than if you sought these services on your own. No wonder, that increasingly, many substantial investors—both individuals and institutions—are now also turning to mutual funds.

Are mutual funds for you?

No matter what your temperament or objectives, there's probably a mutual fund to meet your needs. For example, if you're between investments and need a place to park your cash, there are money market funds. In addition to paying a current interest of about 6%, these funds will also act as a checking account (see Money Market Funds and Money Market Investment Accounts in Chapter 7, for details). If it's income you're after, there are income and bond funds. For growth, you have stock funds. Here you have a wide selection that ranges from the very conservative to the very aggressive. If you want both income and growth, balanced funds are available.

With such a wide array of funds available today, it's possible to establish a complete portfolio of investments using only funds. The first step is to analyze your goals, as you would with any investment. How old you are and how much money you have to invest will play a part in your decision, as will your own willingness to take risk. For example, if you're young and single, you can certainly be more adventurous and go for capital appreciation, while someone on the verge of retirement who must preserve capital may opt for income. Of course if you have substantial amounts to invest, you will have an easier time spreading the risk through diversification. You may build a portfolio of funds, combining ones with similar or varying objectives.

Assuming you have a reserve set aside for emergencies, you're ready to think about what to do with the rest of your money. Is this for the short term or the long term? If it's for less than a year, for example, you may do just as well putting it in a money market fund, especially during periods when interest rates are relatively high. Note, however, most money market funds require an initial minimum investment of $100 or more. (See Chapter 7 for more details on money funds.)

Once you've decided the spare cash you have is for long-term investing, you're ready to ask yourself a few more questions: are you basically a conservative or an aggressive person? How should you structure your portfolio? How much do you want in money market funds? How much should be in stocks and should these be divided into two or more funds? Should some money be in bonds?

Do you plan to spend a great deal of time managing your fund investment by following the day-to-day events carefully and switching funds as the market changes? Or do you just want to find the old reliables, put your money in them, and forget all about it? For most of us, timing the market and switching can be a tricky business. So if you don't want to lose sleep worrying whether you're on top of the market or not, you should seek out funds that are what Sheldon Jacobs, editor of the *No-Load Fund Investor*, calls the solid performers, funds that perform well in both up and, more importantly, down markets. (For more details on portfolio strategies, see Chapter 10.)

The family of funds concept

Mutual funds, like families, come in different sizes. Just as some families are childless, while others have many kids and are still growing, so it is with mutual funds. Some investment companies have only one fund; others have several funds with each covering a specific investment objective. Some *families* of funds, as these are called, have a small number of funds (Value Line has six funds), while others have many and are continuously adding new ones (Fidelity had some 114 funds in early 1987. There's even a newsletter, started by two former Fidelity employees, that covers just these funds).

Joining a family may give you certain advantages, especially if you plan to be an active investor and want a big selection of funds to choose from. You could switch within the family from a stock fund to a bond or money market fund at no cost whatsoever, or at only a minimal $5 service fee. For income tax purposes, keep in mind that such an exchange of shares is considered a sale and new purchase. In a family you don't have to put all your money in just one fund. You could divide it among a number of funds with different goals.

Whether you go with a family or a solo fund depends on your objectives and which fund can do the best for you. It may make sense to have both, as another way of diversifying and thus spreading your risks.

Closed-end or open-end fund?

When searching for a specific fund to invest in, one of your first questions is whether you want a closed-end or an open-end fund. A closed-end fund is one whose capitalization is set, that is, the number of shares available is fixed and there's no continuous offering of new shares or redemption of issued and outstanding shares. Closed-end funds are traded on the stock exchanges with their share prices determined by supply and demand—just like other securities. You even buy these funds through your broker.

Most funds on the market today, however, are open-end funds. These accept new purchases and redeem shares from existing holders on a continuous basis. How much a share is worth is represented by its net asset value, which is calculated once a day by dividing the total market value of all securities of a fund less any money it may owe (liabilities) by the number of shares outstanding. These fund shares are directly available from the investment company concerned or through brokers.

Load or no-load fund?

When you buy or sell a stock, you've no choice but to pay a broker a commission. However, when you buy a mutual fund you have the option of picking a load or a no-load fund.

A load fund is one that charges a commission, which starts as high as 8.5% and declines as the size of the investment increases. A no-load fund, as the name implies, has no sales charges. So if you put $1,000 into a no-load, this full amount will be invested for your benefit. If this same $1,000 is put into an 8.50% load fund, however, the fee is deducted first, and only $915 will be invested.

In your local newspaper, the load funds have two reported prices: (1) an offer or asked price—that's what you'll pay when you buy in, and (2) the net asset value or bid price—that's what you'll receive when you sell the shares.

Although no-load funds charge no fees when you buy in, you should note that increasingly there are some that levy a small charge when you sell. These back-end loads usually run around 1% but can go as high as 2%.

Another recent development: a growing number of no-load funds have become so popular that they became "low-load," by charging an upfront 3% load, or a one-time fee, say $125, to open the account. This trend is expected to accelerate and may become common practice in the near future. Of the 239 mutual fund families tracked by the Wiesenberger Investment Companies Service in early 1987, only 25 have remained true no-loads. These include such industry giants as T. Rowe Price, Scudder, Stevens & Clark, and the Vanguard group.

Meanwhile, of the 2000 or so funds on the market, about 40% of them are no loads. As few of us need more than a handful of funds to accomplish our personal investment objectives, it makes good sense to check out the no-load fund universe first.

Whether load or no load, all funds charge a customary annual management fee of one half of 1% of total net asset value. An increasing number of funds have also adopted what's known as 12b-1 plans. These funds collect an extra fee to pay for marketing and distribution expenses, such as the costs of printing, and mailing, advertising, and paying sales personnel and broker–dealers for their services—items that were previously covered by the management fee. Both charges— for management and 12b-1—are deducted from net assets at regular intervals.

Big fund or little fund?

A record number of investors have flocked to the top-performing funds, making them bigger and bigger. A recent flip through a mutual fund directory turned up more than 30 funds with total assets of over $1 billion. Obviously, the question of whether to choose a big or little fund is one that requires some thought. There are experts who are proponents of big funds and there are others for small ones. Whether big or small, you will find good and bad points about each.

According to an analysis of common stock funds by Gerald Perritt of the Chicago-based Investment Information Services, the smaller funds (those under $500 million) tend to outperform the larger ones. "Being small," Perritt says, "means more flexibility and the ability to concentrate investments" (that is, to hold fewer stocks, without having to commit an excessive amount of money to any single issue).

"Large funds, on the other hand, have greater resources to attract talent," counters Robert Levy of CDA Investment Technologies of Silver Spring, MD. "For example," he says, "they have access to the best Wall Street Research. They may, arguably, be better diversified. Track records are likely to be longer, management policies more stable and predictable."

A number of top-performing funds that received wide press coverage in recent years have taken the drastic step of banning new investors as a way to curb growth. Existing investors, however, may continue to invest in these funds.

With the increasing popularity of mutual funds, it's inevitable that more of them will close in the future. So what should be done if you own shares in a fund that closes? Here too, there is no easy answer. You have three choices: (1) hold on to your shares, (2) buy some more before the fund closes, or (3) follow Gerald Perritt's advice and exit those funds that close their doors and become abnormally large—that is, when total assets exceed $300 million for an aggressive growth fund and $500 million for a growth fund. Perritt adds he'll never rush to buy a fund rumored to be closing its doors to new investors. "I'll pass on that fund," he says, "and look for another with similar investment objectives."

In the final analysis the decision about selling or holding depends entirely on the fund involved and your objectives. For example, if there is no fundamental change and you expect the fund to continue to do well in the future, why not just hold on to the shares? With the new money you'll be accumulating, pick some other fund, possibly a smaller one. That way, you'll get a chance for further diversification.

New funds, old funds, or clones?

With the fund universe growing by leaps and bounds, this is one question investors will increasingly have to tackle when searching for an investment candidate. Let's look at new funds first—with no track records, it is difficult if not impossible to evaluate their performance. "The weight of evidence is against new funds," says Sheldon Jacobs, editor of *The Handbook for No-Load Fund Investors*. In his analysis of all new funds since 1972, over half of them put in a below-average performance rating in their first full year of operation.

Some new funds are actually "clones" of older funds. For example, soon after Vanguard closed the Explorer and Windsor Funds in 1985, they started to offer Explorer II and Windsor II under new management. Some clones share the same management as the parent such as Mutual Beacon or Nicholas II. A March 1986 survey by the *Wall Street Journal* on clones found only 2 out of 11 did better than the parent in 1985.

Whether you go with an old fund, a new one, or a clone, you should spend a little time and check out the following:

1. Know your manager. You wouldn't go to a doctor or a lawyer without knowing something about them. It is the same with your fund manager. What has he done before? What is his track record? What is his investing philosophy? What is the quality of his backup services?

2. Examine the fund's portfolio. For example, if it's a stock fund that you're looking at and all the issues in it are ones that you won't touch individually, than you know this is not the fund for you.

3. Compare fees. Is it load or no load? Or is it a low load? Is there a back-end load? How about redemption fees? How much are the management fees? Is it a 12b-1 fund? If so, how much will this cost you?

Table 8.1 summarizes for you the going rates for these fees.

TABLE 8.1 Summary of mutual fund fees

Type of Fees	Average (%)	High (%)	Low (%)
Load/commission	7.5	8.5	6.5
Low load	2.0	3.0	1.0
No load	None	None	None
Back-end load/redemption fee	1.0	2.0	0.5
Management fee*	0.5	1.0	0.25
12b-1*	0.75	2.0	0.25

*Deducted annually from net asset value.

THE FUND UNIVERSE

There are many types of mutual funds available.

Bonds and income funds

If income is your primary object, you can choose between bond funds, which invest only in bonds, and income funds, which give you the option of investing in either bonds or in stocks with high dividends. In times of increasing interest rates, money market funds are a third alternative.

Stock funds

When you start looking at stock funds, you'll find that within the group called "growth" you can separate them into at least three different levels of risks. Starting with the lowest risk first, you have the growth and income funds, which aim for both current income and capital gains. Then come the growth funds, which stress capital gains rather than current income, followed by the aggressive growth funds, which go for maximum capital gains. Even within the same category, there can be sharp differences in how individual funds are managed. One fund manager may stay fully invested through good times and bad, while another may resort to cash during periods of uncertainties.

Specialized or sector funds

These funds are designed for those who want to invest in specific niches or industries. For example, there are funds that cover individual industries such as banks, gold, insurance, medical technology, and utilities.

Or there are the regional funds, which confine their investments to high potential growth companies in a certain geographical areas, either in the U.S., for example, the Sunbelt; or abroad, such as in Japan.

Then there are the truly international funds, which scout the world for bargains. Unlike the regionals, which are limited in areas where they can invest, these truly global funds can go wherever they want and thus hopefully avoid the bad spots. No matter whether it's regional or global, international funds tend to be more volatile than the domestic ones. The reason: their close ties with the ups-and-downs of the U.S. dollar present an additional risk for investors. The international funds tend to do best when the dollar is declining and the companies overseas are seeing good earnings. No wonder during 1986, the international funds were among the best performers, as you'll see from Table 8.2.

TABLE 8.2 Rates of return with income for international funds

| Fund/
Telephone | Assets
(millions $) | Load
Fee
(%) | Annualized | | |
			12/85– 12/86 (%)	12/81– 12/86 (%)	12/76– 12/86 (%)
Merrill Lynch Pacific (609) 282-2000	445	8.5	77.9	29.6	N.A.
Nomura Pacific Basin (212) 208-9312	53	No	74.3	N.A.	N.A.
Newport Far East (800) 527-9500	3	No	73.4	N.A.	N.A.
G.T. Pacific Growth (415) 392-6181	67	No	70.0	17.3	N.A.
Fidelity Overseas (800) 544-7777	2,561	3.0	68.9	N.A.	N.A.
Price (Rowe) International (301) 547-2000	753	No	60.5	24.6	N.A.

TABLE 8.2 *(Cont.)*

Fund/ Telephone	Assets (millions $)	Load Fee (%)	12/85– 12/86 (%)	12/81– 12/86 (%)	12/76– 12/86 (%)
			Annualized		
Vanguard World— International Growth (215) 648-6000	412	No	56.6	29.7	N.A.
FT International (412) 288-1273	105	No	55.2	N.A.	N.A.
Transatlantic Fund (800) 223-4130	100	No	51.7	17.7	16.0
Scudder International (617) 482-3990	686	No	50.5	23.8	17.8
Trustees International (215) 648-6000	634	No	49.9	N.A.	N.A.
Keystone International (617) 338-3200	90	No	47.9	19.3	14.1
Oppenheimer A.I.M. (303) 671-3408	373	8.5	46.4	19.7	19.6
First Investors International Securities (201) 855-2500	29	8.5	44.9	N.A.	N.A.
Kemper International (312) 781-1121	185	8.5	44.6	21.9	N.A.
Alliance International (212) 902-4000	164	8.5	43.9	N.A.	N.A.
Sigma World (302) 652-3091	9	8.5	43.7	N.A.	N.A.
Pru-Bache Global (212) 214-1230	401	No	43.6	N.A.	N.A.
World Trends (212) 687-5200	58	8.5	40.5	N.A.	N.A.
Europacific Growth (213) 486-9200	160	8.5	40.0	N.A.	N.A.
Paine Webber Atlas (212) 437-2121	225	8.5	38.9	N.A.	N.A.
Putnam International (617) 423-4960	372	8.5	38.0	26.3	19.3
Dean Witter Worldwide (312) 781-1121	346	No	31.5	N.A.	N.A.
Merrill Lynch International (609) 282-2800	278	8.5	30.3	N.A.	N.A.

TABLE 8.2 *(Cont.)*

Fund/ Telephone	Assets (millions $)	Load Fee (%)	Annualized		
			12/85– 12/86 (%)	12/81– 12/86 (%)	12/76– 12/86 (%)
United International Growth (816) 283-4000	205	8.5	28.8	22.4	17.4
Templeton Foreign (813) 823-8712	184	8.5	28.7	N.A.	N.A.
Hancock (John) Global (617) 421-6379	72	8.5	26.8	N.A.	N.A.
Sogen International (212) 832-0022	66	8.5	25.1	22.9	18.5
World of Technology (303) 779-1233	8	No	16.5	N.A.	N.A.
Pax World (603) 431-8022	49	No	8.4	13.2	N.A.
STANDARD & POOR'S			18.6	19.8	13.8

N.A. = not available

Source: CDA Investment Technologies, Silver Spring, MD.

If you're anti-nuclear energy, anti-smoking, or otherwise socially conscious there are also a handful of social investment funds for you to choose from. If you can't find one fund to satisfy your needs, now there are the multifunds–portfolios made up of other funds, either load or no load, chosen by experts. Management fees for these funds tend to run higher, since you'll be paying once to the load fund and again to the multifund managers, in some cases.

In the last year, there has been an increasing number of sector funds appearing on the market. Because sector funds invest in a specific niche or industry and are therefore nondiversified, they tend to be much more volatile than the diversified growth funds, and sometimes move counter to market directions. Gold funds are a good example, as you'll see in Table 8.3, based on rates of return with income during two recent up- and two down-markets.

TABLE 8.3

Name of Fund	Load Fee (%)	Up-markets		Down-markets	
		7/82–12/86*%	2/78–11/80(%)	11/80–7/82(%)	9/76–2/78(%)
International Investors	8.5	16.7	92.0	−26.2	36.8
Lexington Goldfund	No	15.7	N.A.	N.A.	N.A.
Franklin Gold Fund	8.5	13.3	90.8	−28.5	33.5
Fidelity Select Precious Metals	3.0	13.2	N.A.	N.A.	N.A.
Keystone Precious Metals	No	11.2	N.A.	N.A.	N.A.
United Services Gold Shares	No	9.8	102.7	−34.8	48.2
Golconda Investors	No	7.0	N.A.	−26.0	N.A.
Strategic Investments	8.5	3.4	106.1	−33.7	52.8
Standard & Poor's 500		25.5	21.6	−10.2	−12.5

*Up-market is still continuing. N.A. = not available

Source: CDA Investment Technologies, Silver Spring, MD.

Sheldon Jacobs, editor of the monthly newsletter, *The No-Load Fund Investor* advises: "sector funds are not for buy-and-hold investors. Long-term investors are better off sticking to diversified stock funds. If you are attracted to a given sector, limit your holdings to 10% of your equity portfolio." Also, be prepared to switch to another sector or to a money market fund if conditions should change.

The all-sector funds

The time has come when you can simply pick a fund whose assets are invested in the four basic investment sectors—U.S. stocks, foreign shares, precious metals, and U.S. fixed income. The Blanchard Strategic Growth Fund is, so far, the only one on the market doing just that.

As market conditions change, the assets in the four sectors will be revised accordingly. In early 1987, the fund had 29% in U.S. stocks, 42% in foreign shares, 15% in precious metals, and 14% in U.S. fixed-income securities. It's still too early to tell how the fund will fare, as it started only in the summer of 1986. But it should be noted that each sector of the fund is being handled by a top manager with special expertise in that area. All this special knowledge does not come cheap. Although called a "no-load" fund, Strategic Growth requires a $125 one-time fee to open an account, plus yearly management fees that range from 0.75% to 1%, depending on the fund's aggregate net assets, and annual rule 12b-1 distribution fees that may run as high as 0.85% of average daily net assets.

HOW TO GET STARTED

To find the right funds for you requires the same type of research that you would normally do for any investment: take a look at the whole universe, zero in on the ones that seem to meet your objectives, then compare performance over a period of time. Chasing the top performers has its disadvantages, since this year's stars will often be next year's dogs. The reason: funds tend to fall into three broad categories. Those that perform spectacularly well during up-markets; others that bloom only during down periods; and the old reliables. Whether the market is up or down, the reliable ones always do reasonably well. If you're the type of investor who doesn't want to spend too much time managing portfolios, this is where you'll find the funds that will fit your philosophy and goals.

Table 8.4 and Figures 8.1 through 8.8 illustrate how eight of the old reliables have fared in both up and down markets. These include two funds each from the four major investment objective categories: aggressive growth (Twentieth Century Select and Evergreen); growth (Fidelity Magellan and Over-the-counter); growth and income (Sequoia and Windsor); and balanced (Qualified Dividend Portfolio I and Mutual Shares).

TABLE 8.4 Rates of return with income

Name of Fund/ Assets (millions)	Load Fee (%)	Up-markets		Down-markets	
		7/82– 12/86*%	2/78– 11/80(%)	11/80– 7/82(%)	9/76– 2/78(%)
Fidelity Magellan $6,555	3	+34.9	+59.2	+ 7.9	+13.3
Qualified Dividend Portfolio I $177	No	+32.5	+12.8	+16.6	+12.3
Windsor Fund $4,839	No	+29.8	+21.4	+ 5.2	+ 4.3
Twentieth Century Select $1,832	No	+27.2	+51.6	− 6.1	+28.0
Mutual Shares $1,293	No	+26.5	+29.8	− 1.7	+19.3
Evergreen Fund $639	No	+25.5	+51.6	−10.6	+26.9
Sequoia Fund $690	No	+24.9	+19.9	+15.2	+26.8
Over-the-counter $237	8.5	+22.0	+36.5	− 3.4	+25.5
Standard & Poor's 500		+25.5	+25.5	−10.3	− 8.5

*Up-market is still continuing.

Source: CDA Investment Technologies, Silver Spring, MD.

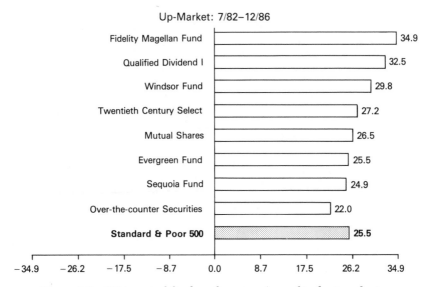

Figure 8.1   CDA mutual fund performance (annualized rates of return with income—7/82–12/86).

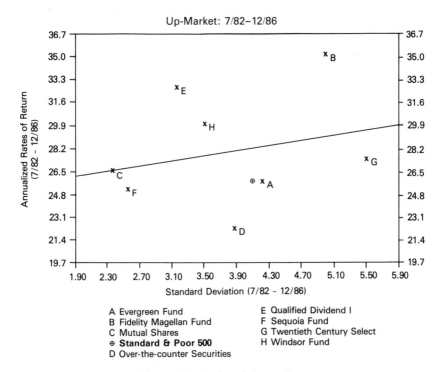

Figure 8.2   Risk and diversification.

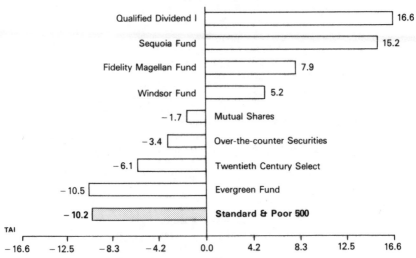

Figure 8.3   CDA mutual fund performance (annualized rates of return with income—11/80–7/82).

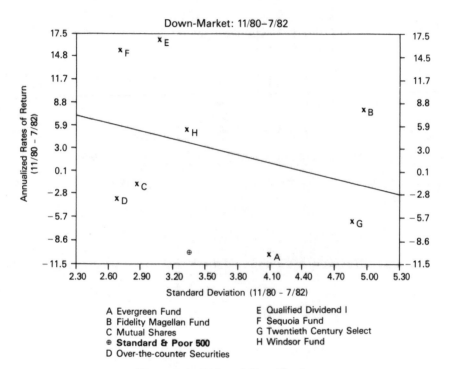

Figure 8.4 Risk and diversification.

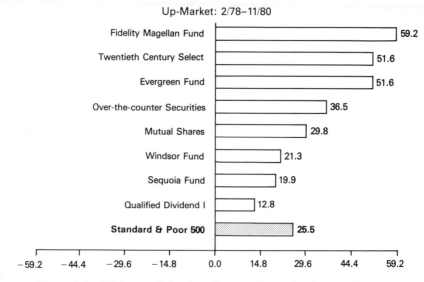

Figure 8.5   CDA mutual fund performance (annualized rates of return with income—2/78–11/80).

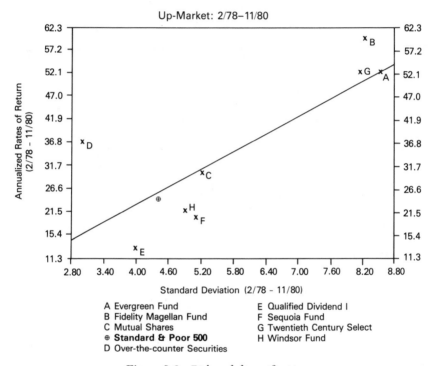

Up-Market: 2/78–11/80

Figure 8.6   Risk and diversification.

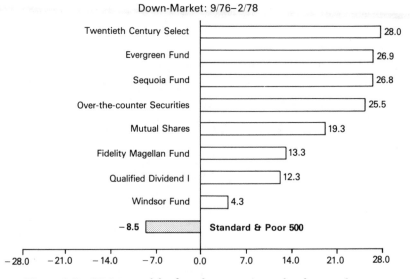

Figure 8.7 CDA mutual fund performance (annualized rates of return with income—9/76–2/78).

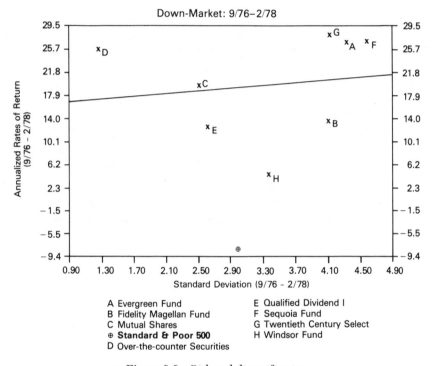

Figure 8.8   Risk and diversification.

How fund managers perceive the market is often reflected in their cash position. In times of great uncertainties, many fund managers will take a more defensive position by keeping a larger amount in cash. For example, during the 1983 market, one fund actually went into 100% cash. "If this should happen again, it's time to give more weight to the middle-of-the-road and conservative stock funds," says Sheldon Jacobs.

Another way to reduce risk is through a plan called dollar-cost averaging, where you buy fixed dollar amounts of securities at regular intervals, regardless of price levels. So when prices are low, you get more shares, and when prices go up again, you'll get less shares. Thus over a long period of time, the price of all your shares will be below average. You need not limit your purchase to just one fund. You can set up a schedule and rotate your investing dollars among a number of funds.

How much will you earn in 10 years?

Using the same eight funds, Table 8.5 shows how an initial investment of $1,000, with an additional monthly investment of five given amounts ($25, $50, and so on), would have grown over a 10-year period.

Why you need a prospectus

Once you've found a fund that interests you, get a prospectus from the fund. This is the document issued by all the funds, as required by the Securities and Exchange Commission, that discloses details on investment objectives, policies, and restrictions; who the managers are, what they've done, how well they did it, and if there are any suits pending against them, plus a complete list of the fund's portfolio. Note, in recent years, the disclosure rules for prospectuses have eased somewhat and many funds are now issuing a shorter version. So when you're asking for the prospectus, also request any statement of additional information that the fund of your choice may have. This will give additional data generally not contained in the prospectus or the annual report.

TABLE 8.5   December 1986 value of $1,000 invested December 1976 plus varying amounts added each month

Name of Fund	Monthly Investment Amount				
	$25	$50	$100	$250	$500
Fidelity Magellan	34,101	51,182	85,345	187,832	358,645
Twentieth Century Select	21,365	32,185	53,824	118,743	226,941
Evergreen	18,138	27,501	46,227	102,405	196,035
Qualified Dividend Portfolio I	17,088	27,710	48,955	112,691	218,916
Mutual Shares	15,493	24,344	42,047	95,154	183,666
Sequoia	15,469	24,471	42,474	96,482	186,496
Windsor	14,991	24,357	43,089	99,286	192,947
Over-the-counter	14,816	22,745	38,602	86,175	165,463
Total investment at cost	4,000	7,000	13,000	31,000	61,000
Standard & Poor's 500	10,984	18,334	33,034	77,133	150,632

Source: CDA Investment Technologies, Silver Spring, MD.

TAKING THE NEXT STEP: WHERE TO GET HELP

Table 8.6 lists helpful contacts that will make taking the next step easier:

TABLE 8.6   Where to get help

Source	What's Available
CDA Mutual Fund Report 11501 Georgia Avenue Silver Spring, MD 20902 (301) 942-1700	Now you, too, can subscribe to a service that used to be for the pros only. This comprehensive monthly report, plus quarterly and annual supplements, will give you all the data you'll need to do the proper homework ($255 a year). Also available is a booklet, *What You Should Know About Mutual Fund Performance*, $10.

TABLE 8.6 *(Cont.)*

Source	What's Available
Donoghue's 1988 Mutual Funds Almanac The Donoghue Organization 360 Woodland Street Box 540 Holliston, MA 01746 (617) 429-5930 (800) 343-5413	An annual directory covering over 1,100 stock, bond, and money market mutual funds. Details given for each fund includes the 5-year and 10-year track records, a risk index, and the investment objective. Also includes the fund's distributor and phone numbers ($23).
The Individual Investor's Guide to No-Load Mutual Funds American Association of Individual Investors 612 N. Michigan Avenue Chicago, IL 60611 (312) 280-0170	An annual publication available at bookstores ($15). Members, who pay annual fees of $48 to AAII, get the guide free.
Investment Company Institute 1600 M Street N.W. Washington, D.C. 20036 (202) 293-7700	A variety of pamphlets, published by this major mutual fund industry trade group. Includes an annual fact book ($1).
Thomas J. Herzfeld Advisors 7800 Red Road South Miami, FL 33143 (305) 665-6500	Tom Herzfeld, whose firm specializes in closed-end funds, is the author of the reference book, *The Investor's Guide to Closed-end Funds,* with monthly updates ($200; book is $25 to subscribers, $50 to nonsubscribers). He is also the author of *High Return–Low Risk Investments* ($4.50, Putnam, 1984)
Growth Fund Guide Growth Fund Research Box 6600 Rapid City, SD 57709	Forecasts on some 40 funds plus how-to articles on topics such as reading charts or compounding, (monthly; $85 a year; $2 for trial issue).
Multifund Investing *How to Build a High Performance Portfolio of Mutual Funds,* Michael D. Hirsch (Dow Jones-Irwin, 1987, $35)	Michael D. Hirsch, vice president and chief investment officer of New York's Republic National Bank, is an expert manager in the use of mutual funds to form successful portfolios. In this book, he tells you how you too can do it.

TABLE 8.6 *(Cont.)*

Source	What's Available
Mutual Fund Forecaster Institute for Econometric Research 3471 North Federal Highway Fort Lauderdale, FL 33306 (800) 327-6720 (305) 563-9000	A monthly newsletter with profit projections, risk ratings, and recommendations ($100 in the U.S., Canada, and Mexico; $115 elsewhere).
Mutual Fund Investors Association 60 Dedham Avenue P.O. Box 385 Needham, MA 02192 (617) 449-8820	Publishes a monthly called *Insight* that exclusively covers the Fidelity family of funds ($49 for 6 issues or $95 a year). Subscription entitles you to a free copy of the *Independent Guide to Fidelity Funds*.
National Association of Real Estate Investment Trust 1101 Seventeenth St. N.W. Washington, D.C. 20036 (202) 785-8717	Publishes *REIT Fact Book* and other material about real estate investment trusts, the mutual funds of real estate.
The No-Load Fund Investor P.O. Box 283 Hastings-on-Hudson, NY 10706 (914) 478-2381	An annual guide on no-loads, plus a monthly newsletter to keep you up to date, including what to buy ($100 for both or $38 for guide alone).
DAL Investment Co. 235 Montgomery Street San Francisco, CA 94104 (415) 986-7979	Publishes the ∗∗*NoLoad Fund*∗x a monthly that divides the fund universe into 6 classes and gives strategies on how to make the most of the top ranking funds ($95 a year).
No-Load Mutual Fund Association P.O. Box 1010, Dept. TP61 South Orange, NJ 07079	You can get an annual investor's guide that comes with a list of the no-load and low-load funds that are members of this trade group (send $5 to cover postage and handling).
Wiesenberger Investment Companies Service Warren, Gorham & Lamont One Penn Plaza New York, NY 10119 (212) 971-5000	An encyclopedia of the mutual fund universe, published annually in a hardcover volume ($245), plus two monthly updates: the *Current Performance & Dividend Record* covering the last 6 and 12 months and the *Management Results* for long-term performance.

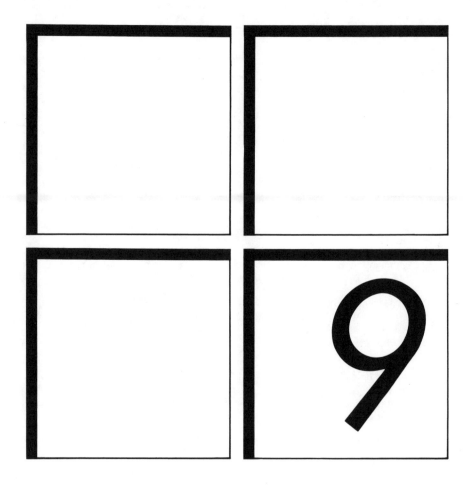

9

Thinking Ahead

Although the present always demands our most immediate attention, it's to our advantage to be aware that one day the future will also become the present. For things financial, it's necessary to think a bit ahead and plan accordingly, or we'll be left completely unprepared. Four areas, in particular, require some thoughtful consideration so they can be linked into our overall plans at the appropriate time.

WHAT IF ...?

Since certain stages in the cycle of life such as living together, marriage, divorce, or widowhood come at different times, many people do not really give these things much thought. That is, not until problems develop. But these problems can usually be avoided, if some steps are taken at the beginning. For example, to avoid future misunderstandings, as when a breakup or divorce is necessary—and recent data shows that, contrary to popular belief, more couples in their 20s are getting divorced today than any other age group—it is a good idea to have some kind of written prenuptial agreement made.

Such an agreement need not be long and complicated, but it must be specific about who owns what. Be sure to include provisions to cover what you have acquired as singles, and for what you will acquire as partners together. One easy way to deal with this: what you have prior to the union, you'll own individually, but what you'll get together will be split 50-50.

As more women join the work force, there will be more two-income families—already more than half the women with children work today. According to the Bureau of Labor Statistics, among the nation's 33 million women with children under 18, 63% work and 72% of these mothers work full time.

A two-income family, as planning goes, provides much greater flexibility but can also be a constant source of conflict unless some kind of understanding is established right at the beginning. Obviously, there are different ways to achieve this and much depends on you and your partner's temperaments, as well as on the type of relationship you have with each other. To get you started on a discussion, here are some suggestions.

Couples who earn approximately the same amount may simply want to split living expenses. Otherwise, it's just fair that the higher-income half should assume a greater share. The first step, however, is to make a list of the common joint expenses. Then figure out how you want to share the burden. Instead of simply dividing the total, you may each want to assume the responsibility for certain types of expenses. For example: the husband may opt to pay for all the house-related expenses, such as mortgage payments, maintenance, property taxes, housekeeper, utilities, and telephone, while the wife pays for the rest, such as food, child care, education, entertainment, and vacation.

Should you have joint or separate accounts? As equal partners, you should probably have both; a joint account for running the household and separate accounts for personal uses. You may want to do the same with your savings and investments: a certain percentage from each partner is put in joint accounts and the rest in separate ones. This way both parties will be protected, and hopefully will also limit the amount of inconvenience or disagreements that may otherwise occur. But more important than the practical aspects of such an arrangement are the psychological benefits. Being able to write your own checks and having your own assets to do with as you wish means independence and with it comes also confidence in yourself.

COLLEGE FOR YOUR CHILDREN

A college education is an expensive proposition today. The average total cost for a four-year public college is about $6,500 a year; a private school is double that at about $12,000. If you want Harvard or Yale, the price is in excess of $17,000 a year. As the current annual median family income is around $29,000, it's easy to see why few families can afford to pay for college costs out of current income. Unless the family has put aside a nest egg for this purpose, chances are it will need some form of outside financial assistance. In fact, an estimated half of the five million students in college today receive some form of aid. Contrary to what you often hear, you don't necessarily have to be poor to qualify for this aid, but you do have to prove you need it.

Paying for college is still very much a family affair and may become even more so, if government aid is cut further. Keep in mind that whatever aid is available, it is always just a supplement. The family is expected by most colleges, government agencies, and private student aid programs to be the primary source of funds—with both parents and students contributing towards this common goal.

How much the parents contribute depends on their income and

the assets they have accumulated. By filing a financial aid statement, their resources will be evaluated against their other expenses, and the remaining available income will be used towards college costs. Colleges usually expect students to contribute at least $700 a year from summer job earnings, savings, or other assets.

The amount of financial aid you'll need may vary according to the colleges you're considering—the more a school costs, the more aid you'll require. Let's say the college you've chosen costs $8,000 a year for tuition and living expenses. Your family can afford to pay $4,000. So your demonstrated financial need is $4,000. On the other hand, if you plan to attend a school that costs $15,000 a year, after subtracting the $4,000 from your family, you'll need $11,000 to make up the difference.

Why not fill in the forms in Tables 9.1 to 9.3 to see how your own situation stacks up?

One thing to keep in mind: the more expensive the school, the more funds they may have to aid students. You are usually eligible for financial aid equal to the amount of your demonstrated need. Whether you get this exact amount or not depends to a great extent on the availability of funds in any given year. The college that accepts you should be able to help you put together a financial aid package.

Outside of your family, there are three types of financial aid available to college students.

1. Grants and scholarships—these are basically gifts and thus the best type to get since you don't have to repay or work to earn them. Grants are usually awarded on need alone, while scholarships may require meeting criteria other than need, such as academic achievement.

2. Education loans—a form of "self-help aid," often subsidized by the state or federal government or by the colleges themselves. As a result, they carry a lower interest rate than commercial loans and generally have to be repaid only after you have graduated or left college.

3. Student employment or work assistance is another form of "self-help aid." The best known example of this is the federal College Work-Study program where students have jobs for 10 to 15 hours a week, and the federal government pays 80% of their salary.

Financial aid comes from a variety of sources. These include both federal and state governments, the colleges themselves, and a wide range of private organizations. Most qualified students get a combination of both gift and self-help programs to form their very own customized financial aid package. The person who can help you most to put this together is the financial aid administrator at the college of your choice. If you think you need financial aid, you should ask for it right at the beginning when you apply to a college. Doing the paperwork early is the only way to find out what's available to you. Some parents are afraid to ask for aid thinking the college will reject their application outright.

"There's no evidence to suggest that happens," says Kathleen Brouder, author of the College Board's College Cost Book. "Saying you need aid is not likely at all to rule out the possibility the college will accept you."

To be eligible for financial aid, you have to meet certain basic requirements. For example, most programs require you to be either a U.S. citizen or a permanent resident, and attend school at least half time, six hours of courses per semester or its equivalent. Programs sponsored by colleges and private organizations may require that you attend full time, which usually means at least 12 hours a semester.

You must also be enrolled in an approved program at an eligible institution. For some federal student aid programs, you can receive aid to attend more than 7,500 eligible institutions, which includes colleges, universities, and vocational and technical schools. State aid programs are sometimes limited only to accredited colleges and universities. Some programs will provide assistance only to study certain areas, such as, religious studies, or in vocational or technical courses where the aid usually lasts no longer than six months.

More importantly, most programs also require that you maintain satisfactory academic progress toward a degree or certification and be in good standing with the institution you attend.

Undergraduates may qualify for a number of federal student aid programs. Some of which are listed here.

- The Pell Grant Program is the largest. During 1987/88, $3.8 billion will be dispensed to 2.9 million students. The grants range from $200 to $2,300, with the average being $1,312. How much you'll get depends on need, the costs of your particular college, the length of the program, and whether you're a full-time or a part-time student.

- The Supplemental Educational Opportunity Grant Program is one of three federal campus-based programs. Although the money comes from the federal government, the colleges distribute the money to students who show the need for it. These awards, ranging from $200 to $2,500, are given only to U.S. citizens enrolled at least half time in an accredited institution.

- The Perkins Loan Program is another of the federal campus-based programs that are administered by colleges and universities. As a freshman or sophomore, you may borrow up to $4,500 a year; a junior or senior may get $9,000 a year, at a 5% interest rate—the lowest of any education loans. Best of all, repayment is deferred until you graduate or leave school, and then you have ten years to pay it back.

- The College Work-Study Program, the third campus-based program, is subsidized by the federal government but administered by the institutions. Based purely on financial need, you may work as many as 40 hours a week, although 10 to 15 is more typical. Depending on your own employable skills, class schedule, and academic progress, you may be assigned to a variety of on-campus jobs—for example, faculty aide, dining-hall worker, library assistant, groundskeeper, office secretary, and financial aid peer counselor.

One way to get a free education is to attend one of the service academies. These are places that train you for a career in the military, Merchant Marine, or Coast Guard. The federal government pays all expenses—you even receive a monthly stipend for incidental expenses. In return, you'll have to accept appointment in the military after graduation. The minimum tour of duty is four years' active and two years' reserve duty.

If you're interested in entering a service academy, contact your senator or congressional representative early in the spring of your junior year in high school and they will nominate you for this honor.

Closer to home, you should also check out the aid programs offered by your state. Ask your high school guidance counselor for complete information on what is available. Most such programs require that you be a legal resident and attend an institution within the state.

One important resource for financial assistance is the colleges and universities themselves. Most schools sponsor and administer a variety of assistance programs. Sponsored financial aid usually comes from one of two sources: tuition revenues and contributions from private donors. Some scholarships and grants-in-aid are based on demonstrated need, while others are awarded on criteria other than or in addition to need such as academic performance, proposed field of study, special talents, or abilities.

In addition to the Work-Study Program, colleges may also offer other job programs, based more on special skills than purely on needs. These might include jobs as lab assistant, business office aide, or dormitory resident adviser.

Short-term and emergency loans at either quite low or no interest are usually available to all students. The repayment period, however, is often confined to an academic year.

As the criteria and application procedures for college programs vary considerably, your best source of information is the college catalog or financial aid bulletin published by the college you're considering. Private colleges often have more college-sponsored aid available to assist you than do public institutions. Proprietary or profit-making institutions generally have very little or none at all.

If you need to borrow money to pay for education expenses, your local bank, credit union, or savings and loan may be able to help. Through the Guaranteed Student Loan Program, subsidized by the federal government, these institutions can offer you loans for under-graduate studies up to $2,625 a year for freshmen and sophomores; and $4,000 for juniors and seniors at a low interest rate of 8%. Keep in mind, these loans are limited to a student's college expense budget minus any other financial aid received. Also, there's an upfront service fee of 5%, which means that for every $1,000 you borrow, you'll get to keep only $950.

With this program, it's the student who's the borrower. So repay-ment on both interest and principal is deferred until the student graduates or leaves school. If parents or students need help for a brief period to solve temporary cash-flow problems or whatever, they can also request an auxiliary loan. These loans, however, have to be com-pletely repaid within 60 days.

Before you dash out to the bank for a Guaranteed Student Loan, it's a good idea to check first with your college financial aid administrator. Why? Some colleges participate in this program as lenders, and in some states such loans can be handled by a public agency.

WHAT CAN STUDENTS DO?

Although the major portion of your financial aid package may come from the joint efforts of college and federal and state governments, sometimes the additional tidbit offered by a private program may make all the difference in the world for you. For example, it may mean attending the school you like best versus one you can afford. So it's well worth your while to spend some time to find out what's out there in private student aid for which you'll be eligible.

- Start with yourself. Look for notices on your school bulletin board and read your hometown newspaper for names of scholarships given in your area. If you think you may qualify, check with the sponsor. Spend a few hours in your library and look through some of the books on financial aid. You may make some surprising discoveries–there may even be a program designed just for you.
- Don't be afraid to ask. Start with your parents. Ask them to check with their employers—many offer some form of scholarship or grant-in-aid to children of employees. If your parents are members of a labor union or trade and professional association, they may discover these organizations have some type of aid available to help members' children.
- Contact your church or synagogue to see if either the local unit or the national organization offers any student aid programs.
- Contact local civic and fraternal organizations, religious groups and veterans posts; many local, state, and national units sponsor some scholarship programs, especially for members' children.
- Investigate programs that may be underwritten by local businesses and industries. Community-based Education Opportunity and Upward Bound programs can sometimes help you in identifying private sources of aid.
- Last but not least check and consult often with your guidance counselor.

Doing the right thing at the right time

One way to improve your chances of getting the financial aid you need is to know what you have to do, when to do it, and how to do it right the first time.

Your first step is to complete a need analysis like the Financial Aid Form (FAF), published by the College Scholarship Service, or the Family Financial Statement (FFS), by the American College Testing Program. Although application requirements vary from college to college, you need generally file only one and have it sent to a number of schools. Your best bet: check with the colleges of your choice first to see which form they require and exactly when these are due.

What is this need analysis form? It asks for information about your family and finances, covering subjects such as income, assets, family size, unusual expenses, and so forth. Before you sit down to complete the form, it's a good idea to have your most recent income tax returns, W-2 forms, and other financial records handy. With this information, the processing agency will analyze and estimate what your family could be expected to contribute toward college expenses. A need analysis report is then sent to the colleges that you specify. You may have this information sent to federal or state student aid programs as well.

Based on this analysis, the colleges will decide how much money to award you. Eventually, you'll hear from the schools you applied to as well as from the state and federal programs. Review all communications carefully and promptly supply any additional information that may be requested.

In the long and time-consuming process to a financial aid package, completing your need analysis is just the starting point. There'll be other forms that you'll still have to complete. Among them will be the college application forms, which are different and separate from the financial aid forms, although you may send them both in at about the same time. Don't wait until you've been accepted for admission to apply for financial aid. If you do, you may find that all the money is gone. If you're applying for a Guaranteed Student Loan, or some state student assistance program, or a private scholarship program, chances are you'll have to complete a separate application form.

How to calculate college costs

"The cost of a college education, which has been increasing at an average of 6% a year, will keep increasing in the years to come," says Jeanne M. Hogarth, consumer economist with Cornell Cooperative Extension. This means if a school costs $5,000 today and your child plans to attend there in five years, the cost then will have increased to $6,691 a year. Sophomore through senior years will cost $7,092, $7,518, and $7,969 respectively, giving a grand total of $29,270.

Parents with young children can easily estimate how much a college education will cost them five or ten years from now by doing a few calculations in Table 9.1.

This is how to use Table 9.1: By multiplying the current four-year cost of the college of your choice by the inflation factor, you'll get some idea of what it will cost you in the future. The sample shown at the bottom of the table is explained here. To attend Harvard or Radcliffe in 1987–88 costs $17,100 a year or $68,400 for four years. Let's say you plan to send your eight-year old son there in 1996. Look at the first column and go down to ten, then move across to the inflation factor—1.79. Multiply the $68,400 by this factor and you'll get a total of $122,436 ($68,400 × 1.79). For your newborn, it will cost even more. In 18 years time, when she is ready to go to college, it will cost you $194,940 ($68,400 × 2.85) to send her there for four years.

Don't let these huge numbers get you down though. With some thoughtful planning, it may not be that unmanageable. To get started, Tables 9.2 and 9.3 will help you tackle two crucial questions: How much is it really going to cost? Where's the money coming from? It's up to you which one you want to deal with first, but let's start with the issue of costs.

First, pick a few colleges that you would like to consider. In Table 9.2 fill in the amounts for the various items and add them up at the end of the column under total expenses. Now turn to Table 9.3 where you'll list your money sources and amounts. When you have that total, return to Table 9.1 and input this number under funds available. Hopefully, you'll end up with a plus rather than a minus. On columns where the total expenses are larger than your funds available, that's when you'll

TABLE 9.1 How to estimate future college costs

			Date completed		
			Date revised		
Years to Go	Annual Current Costs ($)	Total for Four Years ($)	Inflation Factor	Four Years Will Cost You ($)	By Year
1			1.06		
2			1.12		
3			1.19		
4			1.26		
5			1.33		
6			1.41		
7			1.50		
8			1.59		
9			1.68		
10			1.79		
11			1.89		
12			2.01		
13			2.13		
14			2.26		
15			2.39		
16			2.54		
17			2.69		
18			2.85		

Sample:

10   $17,100   ×   4   =   68,400   ×   1.79   = 122,436   1996

TABLE 9.2 How much is it going to cost?

Date completed   ———————

Date revised   ———————

Estimated Expenses

Item	Name:	Colleges Under Consideration				
		1	2	3	4	5
Tuition ($)						
Fees ($)						
Books ($)						
Housing/room ($)						
Board ($)						
Transportation ($)						
Clothing ($)						
Personal care ($)						
Medical insurance ($)						
Miscellaneous ($)						
Total Expenses ($)						
Funds Available ($)						
+ or (−) FUNDS ($)						

TABLE 9.3 Where's the money coming from?

Date completed _____

Date revised _____

Sources and Amount

Source	Amount ($)	Total	Comments
Parents			
Father			
Mother			
Both		$_____	
Relatives			
		$_____	
Student			
Savings			
Summer jobs			
Work rest of year			
Others		$_____	
College			
Scholarship			
Grants			
Loans			
Others		$_____	
Others			
		$_____	
Grand Total:		$	

need to find some alternative sources, which might include some form of financial aid.

What can parents do?

While the student takes care of the research and coordinating the paperwork, the parents should give some thought to how they're going to help with the financing. Actually, the earlier they start on this the better.

However, parents are discovering they're having a tougher time saving for college today since tax reform has repealed some of the more common ways to achieve that goal. By shifting income-producing properties to their children, parents in high brackets used to be able to save a good amount in taxes. With tax reform, any income over $1,000 from such plans will be taxed at the parents' top rate until the child reaches 14 years old, when earnings will be taxed in the youngster's bracket. (For some tips on how to deal with this problem, please turn to Chapters 4 and 7.)

Here are some other ways to pay for college that planners say will work in the post-tax-reform era.

- Home equity/mortgage—if you have a sizable equity in a primary or vacation home, you may want to refinance or get a home equity line of credit and use the proceeds to pay college expenses (see Chapters 4 and 5 for more details).
- A single premium deferred annuity, where the payments are geared to the child's entry to college.
- Zero contracts, where a child's college tuition may be prepaid. The earlier it is prepaid, the smaller amount you will have to pay out. For example, at Duquesne University in Pittsburgh, to prepay for a one-year-old child, who will start college in 2005, you'll pay today about $6,400. But to prepay for a ten-year-old will cost you about $15,000.

   Some 35 states are also studying similar plans. So far, only

Michigan and New Jersey have passed guaranteed tuition bills.

The pitfall with zero contracts is if your child does not attend the school you have a contract with, you'll lose the value of the use of the money that's been paid. If you're considering such a program, you should try to figure out which is the best use for the amount that you'll be paying out. If you were to invest it yourself, what kind of result could you expect? Then compare what you can earn with the future cost of the four years at the college of your choice. Completing Tables 9.1 to 9.3 will help you with these calculations.

Note, on average, college costs have been going up about 6% a year for public schools and 8% for private ones since the mid-1980s, compared with 10% or more during the early years of this decade.

- Zero bonds, or strips. See Chapter 7 for details.
- Tax exempt bonds. See Chapter 7 for details.
- U.S. Savings Bonds. See Chapter 7 for details.

RETIREMENT

With medical advances and more people living longer—and hopefully more useful lives—it's possible that future generations may find "retirement" an outmoded word. Regardless of whether it does become obsolete or not in our own lifetime, one thing is sure: retiring today is different from the days of our parents or grandparents. Today, if there is a mandatory age for retirement, it will probably be 65 or 70 rather than 55 or 60. A growing trend: more people are opting for early retirement so they can go on to a second career.

In addition, we're also more conscious of the fact that finance is just one of several practical aspects of retirement that requires some thoughtful consideration on our part if we want to enjoy it when the time comes. And more importantly, our mental and physical health may actually depend on what we've done or not done to plan for a smooth transition from work to some form of retirement. Here again the question of how well you know yourself will play a big part in what you'll end up doing. Let's take a look at the three most crucial issues.

What will you do upon retirement?

It's a proven fact that to stay healthy both mentally and physically, it's important to keep active, doing what you enjoy. If you wait until the day of retirement to think of what you'll do with your time, it may be too late.

Hobbies, like habits, need time to develop. If you haven't gotten the knack or interest early in life, you may never have the inclination or will to do so. Ask yourself: if you don't have to make a living, what would you like to do? For most people, just playing bridge or golf is simply not enough—at least not over a long period of time.

Fortunately, alternatives abound—it just takes some imagination and possibly a sense of adventure. Think of all the things you would have liked to do but for one reason or another just haven't yet. Make a list of the most attractive ones, noting what's good and bad about each of them. The most enticing thing here is that you can divide your time among several interests, and best of all, you don't have to do anything that you don't want to do. Here are some suggestions:

- Start a second career—do something you've always wanted to do. You only need to do it part of the time.
- Be an entrepreneur and start your own business. Or be a consultant and work only when you want to.
- Go back to school—indulge in courses you never had the time to take.
- Do some volunteer work—churches, hospitals, and agencies, such as the Light House and UNICEF all need help.

Where will you live?

Theoretically, retiring and moving to Florida is a neat idea, but in practice it may not be the wisest thing to do, especially if you have never been there and know no one. If you're thinking of relocating upon retirement, it's best to pick a place that's already familiar to you and preferably one where you have both family and friends. The reason is obvious: with their continued moral and practical support the transition from work to retirement will be less traumatic.

How to finance this new life

When Franklin Roosevelt signed the Social Security Act on August 14, 1935, the hope was high that in the future no American would
need to retire in poverty. Social security payments will help to supplement other pension savings so the golden years can be lived in relative
comfort. However, many people today rely on social security as their
sole source of income during retirement. As Table 9.4 shows, the
payouts are modest. The average monthly benefit for a retired worker
in 1987 was $487; an eligible dependent spouse added $234, and a
dependent child meant an additional $220 a month. After adjusting for
inflation, what a retiree receives today is about two-and-one-half times
that of benefits paid in 1940, the year benefits began. Today, benefits
are automatically indexed to offset the effects of inflation.

TABLE 9.4   Social Security: what you contribute versus what
you receive (minimum and maximum monthly benefits payable
when retired at age 65)

Year	Minimum Benefits Payable ($)		Maximum Benefits Payable ($)	
	At retire-ment	Effective Dec. 1986	At retire-ment	Effective Dec. 1986
1940	10.00	204.50	41.20	395.40
1950	10.00	204.50	45.20	422.60
1951	20.00	204.50	68.50	422.60
1953	25.00	204.50	85.00	466.80
1955	30.00	204.50	98.50	466.80
1959	33.00	204.50	116.00	515.50
1962	40.00	204.50	121.00	537.60
1965	44.00	204.50	131.70	546.50
1968	55.00	204.50	156.00	572.60
1970	64.00	204.50	189.80	605.60
1971	70.40	204.50	213.10	618.10
1973	84.50	204.50	266.10	643.10
1975	93.80	204.50	316.30	688.50
1976	101.40	204.50	364.00	733.20
1977	107.90	204.50	412.70	781.40
1978	114.30	204.50	459.80	822.00
1979	121.80	204.50	503.40	844.90
1980	133.90	204.50	572.00	873.50
1981	153.10	204.50	677.00	904.20
1982	170.30	204.50	679.30	816.00
1983	166.40	186.00	709.50	793.60

TABLE 9.4 *(Cont.)*

Year	Minimum Benefits Payable ($)		Maximum Benefits Payable ($)	
	At retirement	Effective Dec. 1986	At retirement	Effective Dec. 1986
1984	150.50	162.50	703.60	760.40
1985	*	*	717.20	749.00
1986	*	*	760.20	770.00
1987	*	*	789.20	—

*Minimum PIA eliminated for workers who attain age 62 after 1981.

Notes: Assumes retirement at beginning of year when age 65 is attained. For 1983, minimum benefits are derived from transitional guarantee computation based on 1978 PIA table.

Source: Social Security Bulletin, Annual Statistical Supplement, 1986.

In contrast, your social security contribution has been rising, in recent years, at a rapid rate, as you'll see from Table 9.5.

TABLE 9.5 Annual average and maximum taxable earnings and contribution rates under the Social Security Act and Amendments

Year	Average			Maximum		
	Earnings ($)	Rate (%)	Amount ($)	Earnings ($)	Rate (%)	Amount ($)
1937	900	1.000	9	3,000	1.000	30.00
1940	932	1.000	9	3,000	1.000	30.00
1950	1,812	1.500	27	3,000	1.500	45.00
1951	2,078	1.500	31	3,600	1.500	54.00
1954	2,240	2.000	45	3,600	2.000	72.00
1955	2,416	2.000	48	4,200	2.000	84.00
1957	2,569	2.250	58	4,200	2.250	94.50
1959	2,822	2.500	71	4,800	2.500	120.00
1960	2,854	3.000	86	4,800	3.000	144.00
1962	2,949	3.125	92	4,800	3.125	150.00
1963	2,986	3.625	108	4,800	3.625	174.00
1966	3,694	4.200	155	6,600	4.200	277.20
1967	3,791	4.400	167	6,600	4.400	290.40
1968	4,205	4.400	185	7,800	4.400	343.20
1969	4,373	4.800	210	7,800	4.800	374.40
1970	4,464	4.800	214	7,800	4.800	374.40

TABLE 9.5 *(Cont.)*

	Average			Maximum		
Year	Earnings ($)	Rate (%)	Amount ($)	Earnings ($)	Rate (%)	Amount ($)
1971	4,574	5.200	238	7,800	5.200	405.60
1972	5,030	5.200	262	9,000	5.200	468.00
1973	5,628	5.850	329	10,800	5.850	631.80
1974	6,284	5.850	368	13,200	5.850	772.20
1975	6,633	5.850	388	14,100	5.850	824.85
1976	7,190	5.850	421	15,300	5.850	895.05
1977	7,718	5.850	452	16,500	5.850	965.25
1978	8,278	6.050	501	17,700	6.050	1,070.85
1979	9,465	6.130	580	22,900	6.130	1,403.77
1980	10,390	6.130	637	25,900	6.130	1,587.67
1981	11,384	6.650	757	29,700	6.650	1,975.05
1982	12,025	6.700	806	32,400	6.700	2,170.80
1983	12,721	6.700	852	35,700	6.700	2,391.90
1984	13,425	7.000	940	37,800	7.000	2,646.00
1985	0	7.050	0	39,600	7.050	2,791.80
1986	0	7.150	0	42,000	7.150	3,003.00
1987	0	7.150	0	43,800	7.150	3,131.70
1988	0	7.510	0	45,300	7.510	3,402.03

Source: Social Security bulletins.

With social security facing an uncertain future, it's wise to have some alternatives that you can add to your retirement reservoir. Most people who work for an employer, whether private or public enterprise, will belong to some form of pension plan. In addition, employees are often also offered stock or savings plans they can contribute to. For those of us who lack discipline, this is a good way to save since the amount you want to invest is deducted directly from your paycheck. In addition, the earnings on your contribution won't be taxed until you draw on it and along the way you'll also save on transaction costs. If you are currently not in any such plans, check with your company benefits department and see if you'll be eligible for any such programs eventually. But note tax reform is not making that any easier for you. In an effort to be fair to all, the 1986 Act may cause companies to reduce retirement benefits. For example, tax reform has sharply reduced to $7,000 from $30,000 a year the amount of income an executive can stash away in what's known as the 401(K) tax-deferred savings plans.

Helping yourself—IRAs and KEOGHs.   One thing you can do for yourself immediately is to establish an individual retirement account (IRA) if you haven't done so already. Here too, tax reform has left its mark. Under tax reform, if you're covered by an employer's pension plan and your adjusted gross income exceeds $50,000, $35,000 for singles, you will no longer be able to take an IRA deduction. If you are not covered by any plans, or you earned less than $40,000, $25,000 for singles, then you can still claim the full $2,000 deduction, plus $250, if your spouse does not work. In this case, it will bring your taxable income down a notch since whatever you deposit in an IRA is deductible from your gross income. Both your IRA contribution and the income it will earn won't be taxed until you begin withdrawing money after age 59½.

To make things even more complicated, tax reform also allows for an in-between group. If you are covered by a pension plan but your income is in the $40,000 to $50,000 range, $25,000 to $35,000 for singles, the IRA deduction would be proportionately reduced. For example, someone with a family income of $45,000 would now be able to deduct only $1,000, plus $125 for a nonworking spouse.

Even if you cannot take the deduction, you can still make a nondeductible IRA contribution up to $2,000 and defer the taxes on the interest and other earnings until you start withdrawing the account at age 59½. However, if you withdraw before that age, you'll incur an additional 10% in income taxes.

So open an IRA only with money you don't need for daily living or for emergencies. The law also specifies that by age 70½ you must withdraw a minimum required distribution or you'll be subjected to a stiff 50% excise tax on the portion that's less than the law demands.

For part-time workers, an IRA can be a considerable bonus. Say, your nonworking spouse were to take a part-time job, and earn no more than $2,000, he or she can put that full amount into an IRA.

If you can afford to put away money for retirement—whether it's $200 or $2,000 a year—you should probably consider opening an IRA, even without the deduction. You may start your own account, or your employer may have some suggestions to offer as well. Either way, remember it's your own account. So you should study carefully the pros and cons of all the various options that are available.

You may deposit the maximum $2,000 all at once or set up a schedule of periodic payments. You may be able to do it through payroll deduction if it's through your employer. Obviously, the earlier in the year you start your IRA, and the more you put in from the start, the more time there is for your money to grow. In any case, you have until April 15th, the date when your previous year's tax returns are due, to set up an IRA.

Opening an account is a simple affair: just sign an agreement with a plan sponsor and give them some money. You don't even have to file any special forms with the Internal Revenue Service. Just claim your exclusion when you file your regular tax return.

Should you have a self-directed account or have it managed? The answer depends on your interest and how much time you're willing to devote to your investments. In a self-directed account, you'll be your own manager, pick your own stocks or bonds or what-not, and then have a broker execute your orders. In a managed account, you'll let others, such as a mutual fund or a bank, do it for you but you'll still have to decide what it is that suits you best.

Except for the penalty on premature or insufficient distribution, the IRA can be very flexible. For one, you may invest in almost anything, except most collectibles. Under the Tax Reform Act of 1986, the new U.S. gold coin, the American Eagle, will be acceptable for IRA accounts. And your choice of investments need not be permanent. You can move all or part of your account around through direct transfer, where funds are shifted from one type of plan into another. Or you may take a rollover. Once a year you may take charge of your account during a transfer and have 60 days to reinvest that money in another IRA, without incurring any penalty or taxes.

You may also open as many IRAs as you wish, as long as the total annual contribution doesn't exceed $2,000. However, it may be impractical to do so since opening and maintaining accounts cost money. The fees, which are commonly between $10 and $30, may be deductible as miscellaneous deductions on Schedule A of Form 1040 if they are billed separately and are not paid out of IRA contributions. (For details on how they may qualify as miscellaneous deductions, please turn to Chapter 4.)

What investment strategies should you use for your IRA? Broadly speaking, you could aim for fixed income from such things as CDs, bonds, or Treasury bills, or for growth from stocks, commodities, or real estate (see Chapter 7 for details on these investments). Whether to go for fixed income or growth depends on a variety of factors that include

- Your temperament—you must ask yourself: how much risk can I take and still be able to sleep soundly at night?
- Your age—obviously, you can be more adventurous if you're only 25 and have a long way to go before retirement.
- Your overall retirement plan—if your IRA is your main source of retirement income, common sense dictates that you invest prudently. If, however, your IRA is only a part of an overall plan, then you can be more aggressive.

Although fixed income provides you with a guaranteed return, it affords you no protection against inflation. On the other hand, growth gives you a chance for capital appreciation but no guarantee as to what returns will be. As Table 9.6 shows, being aggressive does not necessarily bring you a higher return in the long run.

Where to invest your IRA. Here are some suggestions: ,

- Banks, S&Ls, and credit unions offer an assortment of similar fixed-rate investments with varying returns recently ranging from 6% to 10%. As rates may vary widely, it pays to shop around. Beware of the complex rules governing early withdrawal penalties.
- Insurance companies offer a flexible annuity, which usually has a low guaranteed return, of say 3½ percent, and a higher current rate, possibly 10% or so, for one to five years. Make sure you understand what annual fees and load charges are involved. Generally, it's more cost efficient to keep your investments and insurance separate.
- Mutual funds come in many types (see Chapter 8 for details). Some invest in stocks or bonds or both, others in government securities or money market instruments. Funds may charge a one-time fee to open an IRA and annual charges from $1 to $10. Some may also charge a commission for each trade.
- Brokerage firms offer a complete line of financial services, which includes buying and selling stocks and bonds. So it's the place to go to when you decide to have a self-directed account. There's usually an annual fee, running about $30, plus commissions for each trade.

TABLE 9.6 A look back at the real returns

Investment	Average Compound Annual Returns					
	1 year (1985–1986)	3 year (1983–1986)	5 year (1981–1986)	10 year (1976–1986)	15 year (1971–1986)	25 year (1961–1986)
Stocks	18.6	18.4	19.8	13.8	10.7	9.2
Mutual funds						
International	35.2	22.0	20.8	17.1	N.A.	N.A.
Balanced	17.7	16.7	18.4	12.2	9.5	N.A.
Growth and income	16.8	15.8	18.6	13.9	10.7	N.A.
Growth	15.2	13.1	16.4	13.7	8.7	N.A.
Aggressive	10.5	9.5	14.3	15.7	9.1	N.A.
Government bonds	24.1	23.3	22.2	10.2	9.2	6.4
Corporate bonds	19.8	22.1	22.5	9.9	9.1	6.7
Certificates of deposit	6.4	8.2	9.1	9.9	8.9	N.A.
Treasury bills	5.8	7.6	8.5	9.0	8.0	6.6
Consumer Price Index	1.1	2.9	3.3	6.6	6.8	5.4

N.A. = not available

Note: The figures assume reinvestment of dividends and interest; stocks based on Standard & Poor's 500; corporate bonds from Salomon Brothers, government bonds from Shearson/Lehman.

Source: CDA Investment Technologies, Silver Spring, MD.

• Your employer may also offer you a selection. It'd be up to you, though, to pick the one that suits your objectives best.

• Don't forget the federal government. In recent years it has competed very aggressively for your investment dollars through its massive offerings of Treasury bills, notes, and bonds (see Chapter 7 for details).

What can you expect from your IRA? Table 9.7 gives some idea of what payoff to expect if you were to put $2,000 in an IRA at the beginning of the year for 25 years. Using CDA Investment Technologies' long-term forecast for stocks, corporate bonds, and Treasury bills, the first column lists the investment and the expected rates of return; the second gives you the grand total after 25 years. The last two columns deal with the potential annual and monthly payouts assuming you start withdrawing only the income at age 65 as based on CDA's long-term forecast.

TABLE 9.7   A look at your IRA's potential payoff

Forecast/ Investment	Grand Total after 25 Years	Income at Age 65	
		Annual	Monthly
15.7% Common stocks	$475,312	$74,624	$6,219
9.9% Corporate bonds	193,760	19,182	1,599
8.4% Treasury bills	155,038	12,713	1,059
8.2% Consumer price index	—	—	—

Notes: As of September 1, 1987.

The nondeductible drawback.   Under tax reform if you have both a deductible and a nondeductible IRA, you should be aware that when the time comes for you to start the payout, say at age 59½, any withdrawal will be taxable on a pro rata basis taking into account the ratio of the nondeductible contributions to the entire amount in the account.

For example, over five years, your $10,000 nondeductible contributions earned $5,000, which gives you a total of $15,000. If you withdraw $1,200, $800 will be tax free and $400 will be taxed.

That is simple enough. But if you should have both a deductible and a nondeductible account, then it gets rather more complicated. You'll find the larger the deductible IRA in relation to the nondeductible, the bigger the amount of the withdrawal will be subject to tax.

Let's say in addition to the $15,000 nondeductible IRA, you also have $35,000 in a deductible IRA, giving you a total of $50,000 in both. Under tax reform, if you withdraw $1,000 from the nondeductible IRA, only one fifth, or $200 would be considered from the nondeductible IRA, and thus tax free, while the remaining $800 will be deemed deductible and be taxable.

Is a Keogh or SEP for you?   If you're self-employed, you should also check out a Keogh or SEP (for Simplified Employee Pension) plan. In a basic defined contribution Keogh plan, you can invest every year up to $30,000, or a maximum of 20% of self-employment income, whichever is less. An SEP plan is similar to the Keogh but involves less paperwork.

Another version of the Keogh plan is the defined contribution variety, where you can shelter a larger amount of your self-employment income—sometimes well over half of it. But this is only for those over 50 with substantial income who can afford to make payment every year.

As with the IRA, contributions to Keoghs, as well as the earnings on them, are tax deferred until the money is withdrawn at retirement.

Finances are just one aspect . . .   In recent years, as government has tried to put more retirement resources responsibility on the individual, there's been much talk about how important it is for all of us to save for retirement. At the same time, however, the government is also imposing more regulations and restriction. Witness the Tax Reform Act of 1986 and what it did to retirement planning. Still, many investment advisers suggest workers start saving for retirement as early as possible. With tax laws changing so rapidly recently, it's probably a good idea to be moderate in this regard. Many people may find that when they retire, they may not be in as low a bracket as they thought because they've oversheltered too much income for too long, or tax brackets have been changed to their disadvantage.

ESTATE PLANNING

Taxes haunt us even after death. Currently, most of us with estates under $600,000 may completely be able to escape any federal estate taxes. State estate taxes, however, are another matter, and you should check carefully what rules apply in the state where you live.

One way to reduce estate taxes is to give it away before you die. Each person is permitted to give to anyone $10,000 a year—$20,000 for a couple—without incurring gift taxes. Also, husband and wife have the option of an unlimited marital deduction. This means you can give your spouse everything at death without incurring any estate taxes. In theory, this sounds great. But in practice, it's often not the best thing to do. The reason: although the first spouse to die would have the tax advantage, the second spouse may end up having to pay twice the tax because his or her estate would have grown in excess of the amount in which the estate would pass tax free. It's often best to give the spouse all of the income from the estate, and have the principal pass to the children at her or his death. It may be advisable for medium or large estate owners to give the tax-free $600,000 directly to their children and the balance to their spouse.

Discuss with your lawyer and accountant which is the best course for you.

Wills

The importance of having an up-to-date will can never be stressed enough. Having a valid will is the only way to ensure your estate will be managed by an executor of your choice and only the right people will get to share your hard-earned property.

For example, if you're married, and you died *intestate*, that is, without a will, state law may provide that your spouse will automatically get half of your estate, and divide the remaining half among your children. If you're single, your estate will go to your parents, and if they're deceased, it will be divided among your siblings. It all depends on the law of the state in which you live. So if you have others that you would rather have your estate, then you should say so properly by doing a will.

Making a will is not as complicated a task as it's sometimes made out to be. Some states even accept a *holographic will,* that is, one that is hand written and says simply to whom you bequeath what. But to ensure that you do it properly, you should consult an attorney. Before you do that, complete Tables 9.8 to 9.10. That will give you step-by-step guidelines on what you'll have to do to prepare yourself for this most important task. As lawyers often charge by the hour, the less time you need to spend with them, the lower their fee will be. So it pays to do your homework thoroughly before you consult one.

Getting ready to make a will

Before you go to see a lawyer, you should give some thought to the following three questions.

1. Who do you want to be your executor? Because he or she will be the one to carry out your wishes, it's most important that you pick someone who knows you well and will most likely do what you want. So be very selective. Generally, it's better to have someone not too much older than yourself. It's also a good idea to have a back-up, just in case. Use Table 9.8 to list the possible candidates and their strong and weak points.

TABLE 9.8   Candidates for executor

#1		#2		#3	
+	−	+	−	+	−
Strengths	Weaknesses	Strengths	Weaknesses	Strengths	Weaknesses

2. If you have young children, who do you want to be their guardian or guardians? The ideal guardian, of course, will be one who can supply both care and financial guidance. But often, it's better to have a guardian to take care of the children's daily needs, and another to handle the financial aspects. It all depends who you have in mind for these tasks and what their abilities and talents are. Just keep in mind that the guardian to take care of the children should be someone they know well and like—and who will bring them up the way you would have liked to yourself.

Use Table 9.9 to list your selection, plus what you like or dislike about them.

TABLE 9.9 Candidates for guardian

Names	Strengths	Weaknesses

TABLE 9.9 *(Cont.)*

Names	Strengths	Weaknesses
_____	_____	_____
	_____	_____
	_____	_____
	_____	_____
	_____	_____
_____	_____	_____
	_____	_____
	_____	_____
	_____	_____
	_____	_____

3. What to do with what you own. These can be divided into six broad areas as outlined in Table 9.10.

TABLE 9.10 Asset Checklist

(1) Savings and investments

Dollar Amount ($)	Designated For
_____	_____
_____	_____
_____	_____
_____	_____
_____	_____

TABLE 9.10 *(Cont.)*

_____   _____

_____   _____

_____   _____

_____   _____

_____   _____

_____   _____

_____   _____

_____   _____

_____   _____

_____   _____

_____   _____

(2)   Pensions, group, and individual life insurance policies. These are usually handled separately from your will and your beneficiaries are listed with your employer or insurance carrier.

Pension/Profit Sharing	Designated For

TABLE 9.10 *(Cont.)*

Life Insurance	Designated For

(3) Real properties (house/houses, artwork, antiques)

Item	Designated For

(4) Household effects (furnitures and furnishings)

Item	Designated For

TABLE 9.10 *(Cont.)*

_____	_____
_____	_____
_____	_____
_____	_____
_____	_____
_____	_____
_____	_____
_____	_____
_____	_____
_____	_____

(5) Personal effects (clothing, furs, jewelry)

Item	Designated For
_____	_____
_____	_____
_____	_____
_____	_____
_____	_____
_____	_____
_____	_____

TABLE 9.10 *(Cont.)*

Item	Designated For

(6) Automobiles and other properties

Item	Designated For

TAKING THE NEXT STEP: WHERE TO GET HELP

Table 9.11 is a select list of sources that can help you with information or queries about the topics discussed in this chapter.

TABLE 9.11

Source	What's Available
EDUCATION	
American College Testing Program P.O. Box 168 Iowa City, IA 52243 (319) 337-1038	General information about sources of financial aid and how to apply for it, plus help in filing a family financial statement to find out how much aid you can expect to get toward a child's college expenses.
College Board Public Affairs Department 45 Columbus Avenue New York, NY 10023 (212) 713-8000	General information on financial aid and college costs, also steers applicants to advanced-placement courses and exams.
The Experiment in International Living Box 676, Kipling Road Battleboro, VT 05201	Information about spending a term or a summer abroad studying and staying with a family.
Octameron Associates P.O. Box 3437 Alexandria, VA 22302 (703) 823-1882	Useful series of money-saving primers such as *Don't Miss Out: The Ambitious Student's Guide to Financial Aid*, *The As and Bs: Your Guide to Academic Scholarships* (both at $4.25 each).
U.S. Department of Education Student Information Center P.O. Box 84 Washington, D.C. 20044 (301)984-4070	General information on government sources of student financial aid.
LEGAL SERVICES See Chapter 1.	
RETIREMENT	
National Council on the Aging 600 Maryland Avenue S.W. Washington, D.C. 20024 (202) 479-1200	Deals with issues and national laws that affect older Americans, for example, social security, nursing care, health and housing.

TABLE 9.11 *(Cont.)*

Source	What's Available
American Association of Retired Persons 1909 K Street N.W. Washington, D.C. 20049 (202) 872-4700	A wide variety of services, that ranges from mutual fund investing, group health insurance, to a nonprofit mail-order pharmacy, a travel bureau, and publications, such as a bi-monthly magazine, *Modern Maturity*, and a monthly news bulletin ($5 per year).

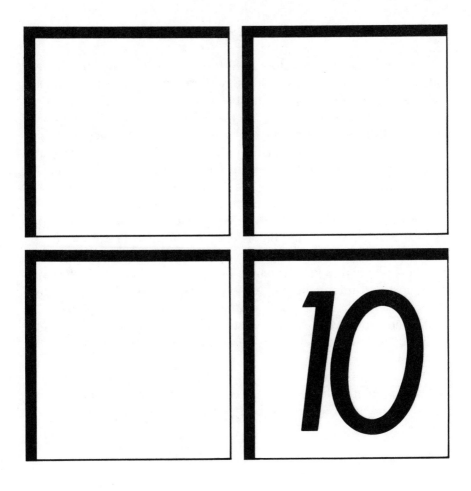

10

*Sample Portfolios
for Different Seasons*

Most successful investors have three traits in common: (1) they follow a consistent investing strategy; (2) they select an appropriate asset mix that takes into account two counter-balancing elements of portfolio performance, that is, the rate of return versus the degree of risk; and (3) they maintain a well-balanced, diversified portfolio that can withstand the vagaries of an erratic market. Just as there are many different ways to invest, there are also many variations to the theme of a well-diversified portfolio.

When you've developed an investing philosophy and a strategy to make that a reality, you'll also have your own ideas as to what a well-diversified portfolio should be. There are a number of ways to diversify. For example, you may structure your portfolio to include a number of different investments, each to meet a certain objective. Your portfolio might include a money market fund for cash, some stocks for growth, some bonds for income, some gold as an inflation hedge, and some real estate as a tax shelter. Or you may concentrate on one type of investment, say, Treasury issues, and diversify by using different maturities.

For small investors, one easy way to get a diversified portfolio is to invest in mutual funds. You can even set up a portfolio of funds and invest in them through dollar cost-averaging (see Chapter 8 for more details).

LEARNING FROM THE PROS

Over a long period of time, as Table 10.1 shows, stocks tend to outperform all other investments. So an all-equities portfolio will most likely achieve a higher long-term rate of return than one restricted to, say, just corporate bonds. But a 100%-stock portfolio will also experience much greater fluctuations and thus more varied results—especially over the short term. So one of the key issues facing every portfolio manager is to establish some asset-mix guidelines that will achieve his or her objectives over the long term, while at the same time recognizing the probability of adverse developments that could result in unsatisfactory returns for certain periods. Ideally, says CDA Investment Technologies president, Robert A. Levy, "the asset-mix guidelines should be premised upon anticipated future returns—not just a continuation of historical results—particularly in view of the higher interest rates and inflation which are likely to prevail in coming years."

With these considerations in mind, CDA has developed a sophisticated asset-mix model the pros are using to help them make this crucial decision. The model includes a long-term forecast for the three major types of investments: Treasury bills, long-term corporate bonds, and common stocks. With this projection—and the use of a personal computer—it's possible to test different asset-mix combinations to see which one will work best for a particular situation.

CDA's 5-year and 25-year forecasts, with the compound annual return and standard deviation, as of September 1, 1987, are listed in Table 10.1.

TABLE 10.1   Getting a long-term perspective

Investment	5-year Forecast		25-year Forecast	
	Annual compound return (%)	Annual standard deviation (%)	Annual compound return (%)	Annual standard deviation (%)
Treasury bills	7.7	1.3	8.4	1.8
Long bonds	9.1	3.7	9.9	8.7
Stocks	14.9	9.4	15.7	22.0
Consumer Price Index	7.1	3.3	8.2	4.5

The standard deviation tells you how much the return may fluctuate each year—plus or minus. So the higher the standard deviation, the more volatile the investment. But over time, these ups-and-downs tend to even out. In short, the degree of risk can be reduced, when spread over a long period of time.

FOR THE HUNDRED PERCENTERS

Tables 10.2 to 10.4 show the probable rates of return for portfolios solely invested in one of the three major types of investments. To read the table, the first column gives the probability starting with zero and increasing by 5% increments. The second gives the percentage rate of return. The nominal returns are what you may earn, while the real returns are adjusted for inflation.

TABLE 10.2 An all-Treasury bills portfolio (compound annual returns for the 5-year period from 8/31/87 through 8/31/92)

Nominal Returns				Real Returns			
Prob-ability (%)	Rate of return (%)	Prob-ability (%)	Rate of return (%)	Prob-ability (%)	Rate of return (%)	Prob-ability (%)	Rate of return (%)
0	4.0	50	7.5	0	−7.4	50	0.6
5	5.7	55	7.7	5	−3.5	55	1.0
10	6.2	60	7.9	10	−2.8	60	1.3
15	6.4	65	8.1	15	−2.1	65	1.6
20	6.6	70	8.4	20	−1.6	70	1.9
25	6.7	75	8.6	25	−1.2	75	2.3
30	6.9	80	8.9	30	−0.8	80	2.8
35	7.0	85	9.2	35	−0.5	85	3.2
40	7.2	90	9.6	40	−0.2	90	4.0
45	7.3	95	10.2	45	0.3	95	4.9
Mean			7.7				0.6
Standard deviation			1.3				2.8

Source: CDA Investment Technologies, Silver Spring, MD.

TABLE 10.3 An all-long corporate bonds portfolio (compound annual returns for the 5-year period from 8/31/87 through 8/31/92)

Nominal Returns				Real Returns			
Prob-ability (%)	Rate of return (%)	Prob-ability (%)	Rate of return (%)	Prob-ability (%)	Rate of return (%)	Prob-ability (%)	Rate of return (%)
0	−1.2	50	8.9	0	−12.5	50	1.5
5	2.8	55	9.2	5	− 6.3	55	2.0
10	4.3	60	9.7	10	− 4.3	60	2.6
15	5.4	65	10.1	15	− 2.8	65	3.1
20	6.1	70	10.7	20	− 2.1	70	3.9
25	6.6	75	11.4	25	− 1.6	75	4.8
30	7.0	80	12.1	30	− 0.8	80	5.9

TABLE 10.3 *(Cont.)*

Nominal Returns				Real Returns			
Prob-ability (%)	Rate of return (%)	Prob-ability (%)	Rate of return (%)	Prob-ability (%)	Rate of return (%)	Prob-ability (%)	Rate of return (%)
35	7.5	85	13.1	35	− 0.1	85	7.7
40	8.0	90	14.0	40	0.4	90	9.4
45	8.4	95	16.6	45	0.9	95	11.6
Mean			9.1				1.9
Standard deviation			3.7				5.2

Source: CDA Investment Technologies, Silver Spring, MD.

TABLE 10.4 An all-equity portfolio (compound annual returns for the 5-year period from 8/31/87 through 8/31/92)

Nominal Returns				Real Returns			
Prob-ability (%)	Rate of return (%)	Prob-ability (%)	Rate of return (%)	Prob-ability (%)	Rate of return (%)	Prob-ability (%)	Rate of return (%)
0	− 14.8	50	15.2	0	− 20.0	50	7.4
5	− 1.0	55	16.6	5	− 8.8	55	8.7
10	1.4	60	17.9	10	− 5.2	60	10.0
15	4.8	65	19.6	15	− 2.7	65	12.0
20	7.0	70	20.8	20	− 1.2	70	12.9
25	8.4	75	22.2	25	0.8	75	14.3
30	10.2	80	23.7	30	3.4	80	16.5
35	11.8	85	26.2	35	4.5	85	18.5
40	12.8	90	29.1	40	5.7	90	20.9
45	13.9	95	32.3	45	6.6	95	24.7
Mean			14.9				7.3
Standard deviation			9.4				9.7

Source: CDA Investment Technologies, Silver Spring, MD.

FOR THE MIXERS

Another way to reduce risk is to diversify into different types of investments—and that's where the question of asset mix comes in.

How do you apportion or divide your assets so that you'll achieve a certain target return? Let's look at Tables 10.5, 10.6, and 10.7—three lowest-risk portfolios for five, ten, and 25 years from CDA's asset-mix model. If your goal is 10% return a year for the next five years then in column one of the first table, you'll find your target return. By reading across that line you'll discover that a mix of 40% in long corporate bonds, 35% in T-bills and 25% in stocks will achieve your objective of 10% a year. But there is about one chance in three that the actual results may be below 7.2% (10 − 2.8) or above 12.8% (10 + 2.8). That's what a standard deviation of plus or minus 2.8% means.

TABLE 10.5 Projected 5-year lowest-risk portfolio for period 8/31/87 through 8/31/92

Target Annual Return (%)	Least Risk Portfolios Percent Asset Mix			Actual Annual Return (%)	Risk/ Standard Deviation
	Bills	Bonds	Stock		
14	0.0	15.0	85.0	14.0	8.0
13	10.0	20.0	70.0	13.0	6.6
12	15.0	30.0	55.0	12.1	5.3
11	25.0	35.0	40.0	11.0	4.0
10	35.0	40.0	25.0	10.0	2.8
9	65.0	20.0	15.0	9.0	1.8
8	75.0	25.0	0.0	8.0	1.2

Source: CDA Investment Technologies, Silver Spring, MD.

TABLE 10.6 Projected 10-year lowest-risk portfolio for period 8/31/87 through 8/31/97

Target Annual Return (%)	Least Risk Portfolios Percent Asset Mix			Actual Annual Return (%)	Risk/ Standard Deviation
	Bills	Bonds	Stock		
15	0.0	5.0	95.0	15.1	6.1
14	10.0	10.0	80.0	14.1	5.2
13	0.0	40.0	60.0	13.0	4.0
12	10.0	45.0	45.0	12.0	3.1
11	15.0	55.0	30.0	11.1	2.4
10	45.0	35.0	20.0	10.1	1.7

Source: CDA Investment Technologies, Silver Spring, MD.

TABLE 10.7 Projected 25-year lowest-risk portfolio 8/31/87 through 8/31/92

Target Annual Return (%)	Least Risk Portfolios Percent Asset Mix			Actual Annual Return (%)	Risk/ Standard Deviation
	Bills	Bonds	Stock		
15	0.0	10.0	90.0	15.1	3.7
14	15.0	10.0	75.0	14.0	3.1
13	0.0	45.0	55.0	13.1	2.4
12	10.0	50.0	40.0	12.0	1.9
11	20.0	55.0	25.0	11.0	1.4
10	50.0	35.0	15.0	10.0	1.0
9	75.0	20.0	5.0	9.1	0.7

Source: CDA Investment Technologies, Silver Spring, MD.

Table 10.8 shows how varying the amount of stocks and bonds in your portfolio over different time frames can affect your overall rate of return. In this example, the portfolio maintains a constant 10% in Treasury bills (T-bills) for three periods—5, 10, and 25 years.

Note, in particular, how a portfolio with 90% in stocks (look at the first row) and 10% in T-bills will have a mean compound annual return of 12.1% for five years, 12.5% for ten years, and 12.9% for 25 years, while one with 90% in bonds (look down to the last row) and 10% in T-bills will return 7.1%, 7.6% and 8.0% respectively. The predominantly stock portfolio has a standard deviation that's more than three times higher than the one with mostly bonds. A more balanced portfolio, say 30% in bonds, 60% in stocks and 10% in T-bills may return 10.4%, 10.8%, or 11.3%—with the possibility of tipping the scale up or down by 6.4%, 4.4%, and 2.7% respectively.

ONE PRO'S IDEAL PORTFOLIO FOR THE NEAR TERM

In early July 1987, Edward F. Muhlenfeld of Rauscher Pierce Refsnes suggested an "ideal" portfolio mix, as shown in Table 10.9, that should last until there is a major change in the inflationary outlook. His objective is an annual total return of at least 15%.

TABLE 10.8 Mixed portfolio (constant—10% T-bills; variable—bonds and stocks)

		Compared Annual Returns					
		5-year period 2/28/85–2/28/92		10-year period 2/28/87–2/28/97		25-year period 2/28/87–2/28/12	
Variable Bonds (%)	Percent Mix Stocks	Mean return (%)	Standard deviation (%)	Mean return (%)	Standard deviation (%)	Mean return (%)	Standard deviation (%)
0	90	12.1	9.4	12.5	6.5	12.9	4.0
5	85	11.8	8.9	12.2	6.1	12.6	3.8
10	80	11.5	8.4	12.0	5.8	12.4	3.6
15	75	11.2	7.9	11.7	5.4	12.1	3.4
20	70	11.0	7.4	11.4	5.1	11.8	3.2
25	75	10.7	6.9	11.1	4.8	11.5	3.0
30	60	10.4	6.4	10.8	4.4	11.3	2.7
35	55	10.1	6.0	10.6	4.1	11.0	2.6
40	50	9.9	5.5	10.3	3.8	10.7	2.4
45	45	9.6	5.1	10.0	3.5	10.4	2.2
50	40	9.3	4.7	9.7	3.2	10.2	2.0
55	35	9.0	4.3	9.5	2.9	9.9	1.8
60	30	8.8	4.0	9.2	2.7	9.6	1.7
65	25	8.5	3.7	8.9	2.5	9.4	1.6
70	20	8.2	3.4	8.7	2.3	9.1	1.4
75	15	7.9	3.2	8.4	2.2	8.8	1.4
80	10	7.7	3.1	8.1	2.1	8.6	1.3
85	5	7.4	3.0	7.9	2.1	8.3	1.3
90	0	7.1	3.0	7.6	2.1	8.0	1.4

Source: CDA Investment Technologies, Silver Spring, MD.

TABLE 10.9 One pro's ideal portfolio

Type	Portfolio Portion (%)		Target Total Return (%)		Portfolio Effect (%)
Mutual funds/common stock	60	×	20	=	12.0
Fixed income securities	25	×	10	=	2.5
Real estate	15	×	14	=	2.0
Total annual average return target (%)					16.5

Notes: Total return equals income, dividends and capital growth. Of the 60% in mutual funds, 30% should be in funds with foreign securities, 15% with U.S. stocks, and the remaining 15% in a Standard & Poor's index fund. Fixed income securities should concentrate on interest-sensitive areas. That can include utilities, income-oriented mutual funds, and depending on your own objectives, taxable or tax-exempt unit investment trusts. The income-producing real estate portion should have a five- to seven-year time horizon.

DESIGNING YOUR OWN PORTFOLIO

Once you have a fix on the asset mix, it's time to decide what specific investments you will include in your portfolio. To help you get started, here are some sample portfolios designed to meet the varying needs of our different seasons. To illustrate how these portfolios are arrived at, we begin with an overview by listing objectives and assumptions. Now you're ready to consider what exactly you'll include in your portfolio: first, pick the type of investments that would meet your asset-mix criteria, then get down to the specific issues. For those who don't want to be bothered with such details as picking particular stocks or bonds, the easiest route to take is via mutual funds. But you'll still have to do some homework to find the funds that will best meet your needs (for more details on funds, see Chapter 8.) The portfolios that follow are just examples, for purposes of illustration only. All target annual returns are rough estimates, based on CDA's long-term forecast. Immediately after each portfolio is a "look back" table to give some idea how the asset mix used in the example would have fared in a recent five-year period.

Spring

EXAMPLE 1: Young single college graduate on first job

Assumptions:	1. no assets
	2. borrowed for education
Objectives:	1. to save for an emergency fund
	2. to pay off education loans
	3. to start building assets
Portfolio:	1. to start, put 100% in high-yielding CDs or money market funds
	2. then 95% in growth/income stocks/funds, and 5% Treasury bills/money market funds
Target return:	15–20% compound annual return

TABLE 10.10 A look back: annualized rates of return with income (12/81–12/86)

Index	Percent Mix	Nominal (%)	Real (%)
Standard & Poor's 500	95	19.8	16.0
U.S. Treasury bill	5	8.5	5.1
Balanced index		19.3	15.4

Put all savings in a high-yield account, for example, a CD or a money market fund. Set a goal for the amount needed in the emergency fund—let's say, three months expenses. When you have that amount, you may consider using the income from your emergency fund to repay your education loans while continuing with your savings.

When you've accumulated your first $500 or $1,000, invest it in a consistently well-performing mutual fund. It will most likely be a growth, or growth and income fund. Continue to add to this with future savings.

Some funds offer automatic monthly investment plans. If you lack discipline, joining such a plan may help. Using the portfolio of eight funds discussed in Chapter 8, Table 10.11 shows how putting aside small amounts over a period of time—in this case, for only five years but every month without fail—can add up to a neat sum.

TABLE 10.11   December 1986 value of $1,000 invested December 1981 with the addition of a monthly investment

Name of Fund	Monthly Investment Amount				
	$25	$50	$100	$200	$250
Fidelity Magellan	$6,669	$9,596	$15,451	$27,161	$33,016
Qualified Dividend Portfolio I	6,463	9,370	15,185	26,813	32,627
Windsor	5,607	8,301	13,689	24,465	29,853
Sequoia	5,329	7,822	12,809	22,783	27,770
Twentieth Century Select	5,237	7,713	12,665	22,569	27,521
Mutual Shares	5,144	7,669	12,719	22,819	27,869
Evergreen	4,777	7,158	11,920	21,444	26,206
Over-the-counter	4,311	6,489	10,846	19,560	23,917
Total investment at cost	2,500	4,000	7,000	13,000	16,000
Standard & Poor's 500	4,946	7,421	12,373	22,276	27,227
Salomon Bros. corporate bonds	5,300	7,839	12,919	23,078	28,157

Source: CDA Investment Technologies, Silver Spring, MD.

EXAMPLE 2:   Young newlywed couple

Assumptions:	1. have emergency fund 2. both work
Objectives:	1. to save for a house or condo 2. to save for children
Portfolio:	80% growth/income stocks/fund 20% bonds/zeros
Target return:	15–20% compound annual return

TABLE 10.12   A look back: annualized rates of return with income (12/81–12/86)

Index	Percent Mix	Nominal (%)	Real (%)
Salomon Bros. corporate bonds	20	22.5	18.6
Standard & Poor's 500	80	19.8	16.0
Balanced index		20.4	16.5

For some planned events in the future, zeros are often a good choice. Pick maturities that coincide with when you need the cash. Also, the income from the emergency fund can periodically be added to the portfolio and be invested in one of the selected vehicles.

Since you are both working, once the common emergency fund has been established, some thought should be given to how future investments should be handled. The ideal situation, when there is enough dollars to go round, will be to have a joint investment portfolio, plus separate accounts for each spouse. Each of you will also eventually be able to set up your own IRA (see details in Chapters 9 and 10 and Tables 9.6, 9.7, and 10.16).

Summer

EXAMPLE 1: Couple in their forties with two teenagers

Assumptions:	1. have emergency fund
	2. own home
	3. husband works full time; wife works part time
	4. children: ages 13 and 15
	5. have group insurance coverage for life, health, and disability
Objectives:	1. to save for children's college
	2. to save for retirement
Portfolio:	40% bonds/zeros, timed to mature for college
	25% growth stocks/mutual funds
	25% growth and income stocks/mutual funds
	10% tax-exempt bonds
	or
	50% bonds/zeros
	25% growth stocks/mutual funds
	25% growth and income stocks/mutual funds
Target return:	15–20% compound annual return

TABLE 10.13   A look back: annualized rates of return with
income (12/81–12/86)

Index	Percent Mix	Nominal (%)	Real (%)
Salomon Bros. corporate bonds	40	22.5	18.6
Dow Jones industrial average	25	22.4	18.5
Standard & Poor's 500	25	19.8	16.0
Shearson/Lehman municipals	10	19.2	15.4
Balanced index		21.5	17.6

Depending on the size of the portfolio, the ideal situation would be to use only the portfolio's earnings to finance the children's education. Or better still, if you have accumulated sufficient equity in the house you owned, you may want to take out a home equity loan. According to the 1986 Tax Reform Act, the interest you incur in this equity line will still be deductible if you use the proceeds to pay for education or medical expenses (for details, see Chapters 4 and 5).

Since you both work, each of you will be able to set up your own IRA and eventually reap double benefits (see details in Chapters 4 and 9.)

EXAMPLE 2: Single parent–mid-30s, divorced with two young
children

Assumptions:	1. settlement from divorce gives her an emergency fund and the down payment for a condo 2. gets some child support 3. works fulltime in a low-paying job
Objectives:	1. to start accumulating assets 2. to improve job prospects
Portfolio:	50% growth and income stocks/mutual funds 40% Treasury issues 10% Treasury bills
Target return:	15–20% compound annual return

TABLE 10.14   A look back: annualized rates of return with income (12/81–12/86)

Index	Percent Mix	Nominal (%)	Real (%)
Dow Jones industrial average	50	22.4	18.5
Shearson/Lehman long-term governments	40	22.2	18.3
U.S. Treasury bills	10	8.5	5.1
Balanced index		20.9	17.1

With young children and a limited income, it's a good idea to have as much liquidity as possible—just in case something happens and the emergency fund is not sufficient to cover. As safety is most important for you, you're willing to forego some return, if necessary, for less risk. But as Table 10.14 shows, you can't go wrong by going with quality.

The goal here is to build a large enough portfolio so that when you retire, you can live off just the earnings, without having to touch the principal.

Autumn

Couple in their mid-fifties

Assumptions:	1. have emergency fund
	2. own home
	3. only the husband works
	4. children all gone
	5. works for company with sufficient life, health, and disability insurance coverage; participates in a company pension plan, which includes a stock-purchase plan
Objectives:	1. to retire in about 10 years
	2. to combine some consulting work with travelling
Portfolio:	50% in growth/income stocks/mutual funds
	30% in zeros/bonds
	10% international mutual funds
	5% or 10% in municipal issues
	5% in gold (optional)
Target return:	15–20% compound annual return

TABLE 10.15 A look back: annualized rates of return with income (12/81–12/86)

Index	Percent Mix	Nominal (%)	Real (%)
Salomon Bros. corporate bonds	30	22.5	18.6
Dow Jones industrial average	25	22.4	18.5
International mutual funds	10	20.8	16.9
Standard & Poor's 500	25	19.8	16.0
Shearson/Lehman municipals	10	19.2	15.4
Balanced index		21.3	17.4

Using the portfolio of eight mutual funds discussed in previous chapters, Table 10.16 illustrates how an initial $2,000 investment with an additional $2,000 added each year in the following ten years, could have grown if left to accumulate. This can easily be an IRA account, for example, where the earnings may be tax deferred until it's withdrawn, starting at age 59½ (for more details on IRAs, see Chapters 4 and 9).

TABLE 10.16 Eight funds and how they grow
(December 1986 value of $2,000 invested December 1976 with an additional $2,000 added each year)

Name of Fund	Assets (millions, $)	Load Fee(%)	Dollar Value
Fidelity Magellan	6,555	3.0	134,247
Twentieth Century Select	1,832	No	83,727
Qualified Dividend Portfolio I	177	No	79,300
Evergreen	639	No	72,572
Windsor	4,839	No	69,518
Sequoia	690	No	67,634
Mutual Shares	1,293	No	67,504
Over-the-counter	237	8.5	61,862
Total investment at cost			22,000
Standard & Poor's 500			53,221
Salomon Bros. Corporate Bonds			46,623

Source: CDA Investment Technologies, Silver Spring, MD.

Winter

Couple in retirement

Assumptions:	1. have emergency fund
	2. own home
	3. have sufficient insurance coverage
	4. belong to company pension plan; also have some of the firm's common stock
	5. receive social security.
Objectives:	1. to maintain similar lifestyle
	2. to travel and see the world
Portfolio:	25% income/growth stocks/mutual funds
	25% growth stocks/mutual funds
	25% in Treasury/corporate bonds
	25% Treasury bills
Target return:	15–20% compound annual return

TABLE 10.17 A look back: annualized rates of return with income (12/81–12/86)

Index	Percent Mix	Nominal (%)	Real (%)
Salomon Bros. corporate bonds	25	22.5	18.6
Dow Jones industrial average	25	22.4	18.5
Standard & Poor's 500	25	19.8	16.0
U.S. Treasury bill	25	8.5	5.1
Balanced index		18.3	14.5

Retirement income comes from four major sources: company pension program, social security, IRA, and other savings. The ideal personal portfolio has sufficient funds to generate enough income for you to live on so you need never touch the principal.

RETROSPECTIVE

In the course of the last 15 years, the financial markets went through two separate eras. In the 1970s, the Organization of Petroleum Exporting Countries (OPEC) generated oil price rise shock created soaring inflation that made tangible assets such as commodities and collectibles the winning investments. Then in the 1980s, low inflation and interest rates put financial assets such as stocks and bonds on top.

Table 10.18, compiled by Salomon Brothers, shows how various tangible and financial assets performed against the CPI over the last 1, 5, 10, and 15 years. During the full 15-year period, the top five items were all tangible assets, led by U.S. coins with an 18.8% compound annual rate of return, followed by oil at 13.9%, stamps at 13.6%, gold at 11.9%, and silver at 10.3%. With interest rates at record highs during this period, Treasury bills (ranked number 6 with a 9.20 percent return) outperformed both bonds (number 8 with 8.70%) and stocks (number 9 with 8.60%). But in the past five years, common stocks took the lead with a 24.1% compound annual rate of return, followed by bonds, at 19.7%. Treasury bills remained at number 6, with an 8.5% return. The biggest loser was U.S. farm land, whose returns fell far short of inflation in all four periods.

What is obvious from this 15-year retrospective is that there is no one winning investment for all seasons. The best way to protect yourself is by diversifying and designing a balanced portfolio with the proper asset mix to meet your target objective.

TABLE 10.18 A 15-year retrospective—compound annual rates of return from June 1972 to June 1987

Rank	Investment	15 years	Investment	10 years	Investment	5 years	Investment	1 year
1	U.S. coins	18.80	Stocks	16.30	Stocks	24.10	Silver	39.80
2	Oil	13.90	Bonds	13.90	Bonds	19.70	Gold	29.10
3	U.S. stamps	13.60	U.S. coins	11.80	U.S. coins	11.40	Oil	27.40
4	Gold	11.90	Chinese ceramics	11.30	Diamonds	10.20	Foreign exchange	25.00
5	Silver	10.30	Treasury bills	10.20	Old masters	9.50	Stocks	20.60
6	Treasury bills	9.20	Bonds	9.70	Treasury bills	8.50	U.S. coins	10.70
7	Old masters	9.20	Old masters	9.70	Gold	6.80	Old masters	8.60
8	Bonds	8.70	Silver	9.70	Foreign exchange	6.80	Diamonds	7.00
9	Stocks	8.60	Gold	9.20	Housing	4.80	Housing	6.80
10	Chinese ceramics	8.30	Diamonds	8.90	Silver	4.00	Chinese ceramics	6.70
11	Housing	8.20	Housing	7.40	CPI	3.50	Treasury bills	5.70
12	CPI	6.90	CPI	6.50	Chinese ceramics	3.40	Bonds	5.70
13	U.S. farm land	6.30	Foreign exchange	4.10	U.S. stamps	-1.30	CPI	3.80
14	Foreign exchange	4.60	Oil	3.00	U.S. farm land	-7.80	U.S. stamps	0.50
15	Diamonds	4.10	U.S. farm land	1.50	Oil	-11.80	U.S. farm land	-7.90

Notes: All returns are for the period ended June 1, 1987, based on latest available data. CPI = Consumer Price Index.
Source: Salomon Brothers.

Index

Pauline Tai
P. O. Box 6356 FDR Station
New York, NY 10150

Dear Friend,

If you've arrived at this page, chances are you have just finished reading this book. I hope you enjoyed it, as much as I did in writing it for you. In an effort to serve you better in the future, I'd like to hear from you. For your convenience, the few questions below will get you started.

I appreciate your interest very much and look forward to hearing from you.

  * * * * * * *

1. What is your overall impression of the book? What areas would you like to see expanded? Are there any other topics that you'd like included? _____

_____

_____

2. I am currently working on the second part to this book: a workbook that will include not only investment-type information, but also personal data, ranging from family medical history to lists of household effects. When you complete this workbook, you will have at your finger tips your own life data book. For those with PCs, a software program will also be available on this workbook.

Will you be interested in such a workbook? If yes, the workbook or the software? _____

_____

3. If an annual update is available covering the various financial markets (savings, mutual funds, stocks, bonds, etc.), would you be interested in such a roundup? _____

_____

4. Other comments: _____

_____

_____

Name: _____ Tel: _____
Address: _____

_____